Group Power

David L. Williamson has been actively involved as a participant and leader in small groups for more than twenty years. He has written several articles about support groups, and he teaches courses and workshops on small-group leadership in a variety of settings.

GROUP POWER

How to Develop, Lead,
and Help Groups Achieve Goals

David L. Williamson

Prentice-Hall, Inc., Englewood Cliffs, New Jersey 07632

Library of Congress Cataloging in Publication Data

Williamson, David L. (David Louis), 1937–
  Group power.

  "A Spectrum Book."
  Bibliography: p.
  Includes index.
  1. Small groups. 2. Leadership.
HM24.W49   302.3'4   81–13849
                                 AACR2

ISBN 0-13-365437-0

ISBN 0-13-365429-X

This Spectrum Book is available to businesses and organizations
at a special discount when ordered in large quantities. For
information, contact Prentice-Hall, Inc., General Book Marketing,
Special Sales Division, Englewood Cliffs, N.J. 07632.

Cover design by Velthaus & King

Prentice-Hall International, Inc., *London*
Prentice-Hall of Australia Pty., Limited, *Sydney*
Prentice-Hall of Canada, Ltd., *Toronto*
Prentice-Hall of India Private, Limited, *New Delhi*
Prentice-Hall of Japan, Inc., *Tokyo*
Prentice-Hall of Southeast Asia Pte., Ltd., *Singapore*
Whitehall Books Limited, *Wellington, New Zealand*

To Anne and to Mark, Suzanne, and Sara,
my most important and dearest small group,
who have continued to love,
encourage, and inspire me through it all!

Contents

Preface

Presented in the pages of this book is a summary of small group dynamics and leadership skills arranged in a developmental framework and applicable to a wide variety of small groups. In the pages that follow, the reader will be able to identify the group goals, group dynamics, leadership goals, and leadership skills that are operative at each of the four distinct developmental stages of the group's history and development. What is operative and effective in a beginning small group differs from that which is operative and effective in a group that has met regularly for a moderate to long period of time.

The reader (small group leader, potential leader, group participant) will be provided with a basic understanding of group dynamics and leadership skills that have been discovered and/or affirmed through extensive research in both group and individual counseling and psychotherapy. Furthermore, it is assumed that these dynamics and skills are transferable and applicable to most small groups. Nearly all groups have similar interpersonal dynamics operating within the group, and similar leadership skills are needed in working with the group participants. Thus, psychotherapy groups, counseling groups, education, study, or skill development groups, task forces, team-building groups, participatory management groups, and the like—all these groups experience similar dynamics as people meet and work with one another over a period of time. Although most of the literature focuses on the dynamics and leadership of a particular group, this book is designed to be applicable to leaders and participants in all kinds of small groups. It is intended to represent a middle ground between the technical literature coming out of psychotherapeutic research and the simplified "how to" manuals written for a narrow and specific kind of group.

Furthermore, this book is written for both the nonprofessional and the helping professional person as they exercise a leadership role in a small group. It is my hope that the technical literature will find a specific application and usefulness to this wide range of purposes for which small groups are formed. Thus, the concepts presented here are useful to people involved with small groups in educational settings (most classrooms are small groups), business and industry, health care and professional organizations, community and religious organizations, as well as counseling and psychotherapy settings.

Exercises are provided at the end of each chapter so that the reader who is using this text in a classroom, workshop, or study group setting can experience some of the dynamics and practice some of the leadership skills that are discussed. Since we learn better when we are active in the learning, experiencing the dynamics, trying on new behavior, skill practice, and role playing sessions will increase the effectiveness of the learning experience. If, in addition, the reader can observe a highly effective group leader modeling the skills that are discussed in this book, the reader's learning experience will be enhanced.

This book also makes an effort to weave together in the developmental framework the understanding of group dynamics with the skills that research in individual counseling and psychotherapy have found to be important in the helping person (counselor, therapist, or paraprofessional). It is the be-

lief that what is helpful in a one-to-one interpersonal and helping relationship is also important to the effective leadership
of a small group, particularly in an awareness of and in facilitating the interpersonal dynamics operating within that group.

Although many people have contributed to this project—
my professors, mentors, friends, colleagues, counselees, and
researchers and writers in this field, and certainly my family—
I am especially grateful to the students to whom I've taught
the material, particularly the support given by lay group leaders at the Colonial Church of Edina and by college students
at a small group leaders workshop at IVCF's Bear Trap Ranch.
They have challenged and encouraged me to put a course
outline into manuscript form. I am also very appreciative of
Mary Kennan of Prentice-Hall, who believed this was useful
material and encouraged the effort involved in writing this
manuscript. And certainly my secretary, Judy Olson, who
typed and retyped the manuscript, giving enthusiastic support
all the way, even when it meant retyping sections and facing
the pressures of deadlines, deserves thanks. She was helped
by the rest of the Colonial secretarial staff ("the working"
staff) in the process. To each of them, I am grateful.

Group Power

The Emergence and Importance of Small Groups

Groups, groups, groups—it seems that wherever one looks in our contemporary society there are groups. Some of these groups are very large, others quite small, and it has been particularly the small group that has experienced a new appreciation, and expanded utilization and greater participation in the past twenty years. The small group movement grew almost dramatically in the late '60s and early '70s as people "discovered" and "experienced" the particular contributions, pleasures, and potential power of small groups—from psychotherapy groups to community action and social change groups, from personal growth groups to Bible study and prayer groups, from corporate team building to support groups for people experiencing stress, from chemical dependency treatment groups to self-awareness groups, and so on. Being a member of a group (a "groupie") virtually became a way of life for many.

Some of the fuel that powered the development of the small group movement came from a reaction against the rugged individualism and frontier mentality of the years of western expansion in the United States, from a renewed appreciation for community, and from a recognition of the intrinsic value of people meeting together and developing mutually supportive relationships. Yet, at the same time, there were other forces that created small groups. Participants discovered, almost accidentally, that in groups there was considerable power at work to effect major accomplishments. There were many reasons for the rather sudden upsurge of interest in groups. In more recent years, the small group movement, while remaining strong, has encountered the voices of criticism and reaction through sarcastic, humorous put-downs of "groupies" or a renewed emphasis on either the individual or the larger social units. Nonetheless, the small group movement continues to flourish as an effective vehicle for achieving both personal, organizational, and societal goals.

Historical Backgrounds

Although the modern small group movement is rather young, the small group has been a significant, important phenomenon throughout history. The religious communities of the ancient world often found their prime expression in and through small gatherings of the faithful, particularly in ancient Judaism and in the early Christian church. Throughout the history of the church, small groups have played an important role in religious renewal movements such as the early monasticism of the third and fourth century, the Oxford Group in England which helped stimulate the Evangelical Revival and its social ramifications, and in the Great Awakening in America. The modern missionary movement of the Christian church emerged in part from the Student Christian Movement of the late 1800s, which was to a large extent a small group movement.

More recently, small groups have demonstrated their effectiveness and importance in a wide variety of interesting ways. The contemporary surge of interest in small groups grew, to a considerable extent, out of the field of psychotherapy. Classic, traditional psychiatry and psychotherapy were practiced in a one-to-one relationship between doctor and client or therapist and client, with primary attention given to inner-psychic phenomena trying to provide insight and understanding so that with the client's personal awareness and intrinsic motivation to avoid pain, change, and growth could occur. Or at least clients could come to a more satisfying acceptance of their difficulties. Eventually medical treatment programs became more sophisticated and effective ways of treating mental health clients. Behavioral psychology emerged first as a research and data gathering process and then as a means of treatment. Virtually all of these were one-to-one, doctor–patient treatment approaches. However, economics entered the picture. One-to-one psychiatry and psychotherapy was expensive and therefore not readily available to the masses of middle-income working-class persons who needed help. Particularly critical was the economics of working with hospitalized patients, especially the state hospitals where public funds for mental health issues were frequently in short supply. Thus the emergence of group counseling, where several hospital patients or out-patient clients could meet together and share the cost of professional time and services.

An interesting phenomenon was observed in that experiment. What began as a pragmatic, economic strategy became an effective tool for helping those who participated in the groups. Not only was it more economical to work with people in groups, it was frequently more effective. Rather than impede the client's progress in going from a one-on-one therapeutic relationship to a small group, it often stimulated the progress. Many group members improved faster than non-group members. The group itself seemed to have an instrinsic therapeutic value for the group members. Indeed, for many people group therapy became the treatment of choice.[1] Small groups can and do have powerful therapeutic effect.

A parallel development has been the use of small groups for the treatment and support of chemically dependent persons. Since its beginnings in the late 1930s and early 1940s, Alcoholics Anonymous (AA) has demonstrated great effectiveness in helping alcoholics, and now persons dependent on other chemicals gain and retain their sobriety. In fact, recent studies have suggested that regular participation in an AA

---

[1] See Irwin Yalom, *The Theory and Practice of Group Psychotherapy*, 2nd ed. (New York: Basic Books, 1975), for summaries and references to the extensive research from which these conclusions were drawn.

group is the most important ingredient in the treatment process of chemically dependent people. AA is, of course, a small group and, incidentally, led entirely by nonprofessionals!

Small Group Contributions in Varied Settings

Reflecting on other places where small groups have been utilized, we notice that small groups have made important contributions in a variety of settings. The space program of the United States is very fascinating, not only in what it has accomplished (watching, by way of television, Neil Armstrong walk on the moon was thrilling almost beyond belief!), but also in terms of the process by which such a tremendous achievement could be accomplished. Thousands of people, from brilliant, creative scientists to skilled technicians and office secretaries, coordinated by competent managers, played important roles and made significant contributions to the various space projects. Yet, throughout this massive effort, the thousands of pieces of work that eventually were brought together for the successful flight were virtually all accomplished by small groups working together in a spirit of collaborative teamwork. Were it not for the hundreds of small groups functioning effectively, it is doubtful that the moon landing, the photographs of Mars or Saturn, or the other space program projects could have been accomplished.

The team approach of the space program and the small task force orientation of space technology has been transferred both to other fields of technology and to business management approaches as well. Again and again, the small-group approach has demonstrated its usefulness to business and industry and has been reflected in team-building workshops, appointment of task forces, and an increase in participatory or cooperative management styles.

In reflecting on social changes that have occurred in America's history, we see another area where small groups have had an impact. These groups often link together and form a network through which the small groups can effect enormous impact on social structures. Labor unions, for example, evolved from small groups joined together by a common concern. The Civil Rights movement of the 50s and the anti-Viet Nam War movement of the early 70s were fanned by countless little groups around the country, meeting and working together toward a common goal. Today, while heavily emphasizing the impact of television, America's political parties still view the neighborhood coffees and the precinct caucuses as the backbone of American politics.

Furthermore, professional athletic teams have demonstrated again and again that it takes more than great individual talent for a team to win a championship. The presence of several high-priced superstars on one team does not create a world championship. It takes something more—a team of athletes working together effectively, a highly functioning small group, if you will. Hear the slogans: "40 for 60," "We are family," "We love each other," emerging from the championship locker rooms.

Small Groups Fill a Personal Need

Finally, there seems to be a strong desire for people to experience community and in-depth relationships. In our technological, uprooted, mobile, impersonal, mass-oriented, contemporary society, the complementary needs for solitude, intimacy, privacy, and a few significant relationships emerge as universal needs. We have a need to belong, not to an undifferentiated mob, but to a handful of people with whom we can share our thoughts and feelings and with whom we can work to create something of lasting value. The small group experience, if it is effective and appropriate, can provide part of that need.

Psychology, industry, social history, theology, and religious history—all concur—groups are important. It is the purpose of this book to provide the reader with a basic introduction to the dynamics of a small group and to the leadership skills that are important to proficiently lead a small group. It is offered with the hope that this material can be applied in a wide variety of settings: support and personal growth groups (where this writer has been deeply involved), task force groups, team-building groups in business, industry, and the professions, study and educational groups, religious groups, group counseling, and so on. While the settings and purposes for which these groups are formed vary greatly, the dynamics of nearly all small groups are very similar. Also, while there are aspects of leadership that differ from one kind of group to another, there is a basic core of leadership skills that is operative in most group settings. Therefore, nearly anyone involved in leading a small group, as well as many participants of small groups, should find this material useful.

A PSYCHOLOGY OF GROUPS—AN OVERVIEW

The Context of Personality Formation

Groups are important because we have discovered or rediscovered that personality is formed and shaped in the context of a small group—the family. We become what we are largely, if not totally, through our contact and involvement with others. Furthermore, we can be and often are reshaped through our involvement with others, usually in a small, intimate context. We are social creatures and have a need to belong to someone, or better—a group of "someones." It is here that healing, growth, new life, and new discoveries can be experienced in relation to others. It has been said, "By the crowd we have been broken, by the crowd we are healed"; John Donne declared that "no man is an island." We are social creatures. We learn in part by observing and by mimicking, by trying on a role, and by experience as we become aware of the way others respond, not only to us, but to each other.

Efficiency and Power

Furthermore, small groups are both more efficient and more potent. Psychiatrists and psychotherapists found they could work with six to eight people in a group that met for an hour and a half to two hours. To work with them individually would take six to eight hours. There is economic efficiency in the use of time. There is also more power in a group. In a small group, the total energy resource and power available is greater than the sum of the parts. A group of six persons has more power than the total of those six individuals acting indepen- dently or in one-on-one relationships (dyads). This can be seen diagramatically, noting that a leader meeting with six individu- als has six relationships as a result of contact with those six people individually.

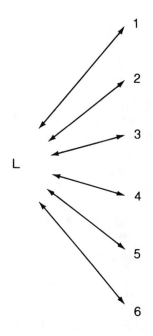

FIGURE 1   (⟷ one to one relationship)

With those same six persons in a group, there are twenty- one relationships as a result of a leader's contact with those six people:

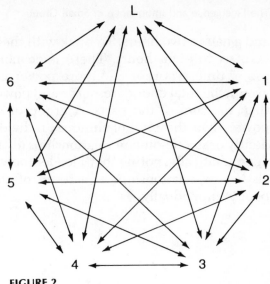

FIGURE 2

Which diagram appears to contain more energy and power? There is more stimulation, there are more ideas, and therefore, there is greater creativity in small groups than in individual working relationships. There are more models for the participant to observe and learn from. Furthermore, in a group, the nonverbal person can participate by observing, mimicking, listening, and so on. In a typical one-on-one helping relationship, the nonverbal or inarticulate person gains very little.

Part of the power or energy comes as leadership is shared in the group with several participants functioning from time to time as leaders. They all have a share in the responsibility for the group and creatively manage its energy. A primary task, then, of the group leader is to help channel that energy and orchestrate that power in a constructive way.

Lifelike

Groups are effective in providing help to individuals because they are more lifelike. We live in the context of many relationships and several groups (family, work, community, church, clubs, teams, etc.). Thus, learning and growth that occurs in a small group are more likely to transfer to the other settings

8

of a person's life than that which occurs in a one-on-one relationship. A further advantage to interpersonal groups is that they help the participant avoid self-absorption. People in a group are encouraged and challenged to be aware of, interested in, and concerned with the other people in the group. It is much more difficult for a person to withdraw and become self-involved in the context of a group than in a private relationship. Part of the involvement with others comes as people respond to the needs of others and as group members help each other, stimulating and challenging the further growth of each participant. The newly learned behavior can then be transferred to situations outside the group.

Limitations and Disadvantages

It should be noted that our enthusiasm for small groups can lead us to oversell the small group experience such that participants become frustrated or discouraged when difficulties are encountered. Simply gathering a group together does not automatically guarantee success. Even when the dynamics are clearly understood and the leadership skills carefully and competently exercised, there is no guarantee that the group will achieve its purpose to the satisfaction and delight of all concerned. Groups are nearly as varied and unpredictable as individuals.

Then too, there are a few disadvantages to groups. First, many people are reluctant to be open or cooperative in a group, especially in a group of peers. Thus, particularly in therapy, support, or growth groups, but also in team-building and task-oriented groups, potential members may be reluctant to join; those who are a part of the group may resist, even tenaciously, being vulnerable and open because of fear of rejection by the others in the group. In addition, the small group is often perceived by the potential participant as impersonal, inattentive, and therefore not as valuable or effective. A third disadvantage is due to the greater resources present in a group. At times, a group member may feel overwhelmed and worn out by all the energy that surfaces in a group, and a kind of "burn out" or lethargy may be experienced. And, with the greater numbers, a small group may get bogged down by having so many people involved stating or expressing their needs, ideas, leadership, and so on.

KINDS OF GROUPS

The different kinds of small groups that can exist are as numerous and varied as the imagination. They can exist for a variety of purposes with widely differing styles of group life and of leadership approaches. They can vary in size from two or three to quite large "small" groups (generally speaking, the discussion in this book is for groups of five to twenty-five people). There are, first of all, work- and task-oriented groups in business, industry, and in community or religious organizations. They can exist as committees, boards, or task forces for the purpose of publishing the college yearbook, writing a proposal for securing a federal grant, putting together a new advertising campaign for a client, and so on. Second, there are educational or study groups designed to build a knowledge or skill base for the participants such as a communications workshop, a Bible study group, or a Boy Scout troop. Third, there are social groups whose primary function is to provide social contact, for example, bridge clubs, ski groups, and so on. Fourth are what can be referred to as support groups, groups that meet to offer encouragement and support as members utilize their own resources to effectively cope with particular stresses in their lives, for example, AA, people going through grief, in job transition, experiencing divorce, coping with cancer, and so on. Also, there are counseling and growth groups where the focus is on both the support and the building of new insights and new behaviors that will result in personal and interpersonal growth. Lastly, there are psychotherapy groups aimed at helping people restructure their thinking, feelings, and/or behavior, that is, to reshape their personalities in order to live more effective and satisfying lives. In practice, groups are often a combination of two or more of these kinds of groups. The greater the combination is, the less clear the purpose becomes, the more complex the dynamics are, and the more difficult the leadership function is.

KINDS AND STYLES OF LEADERSHIP

To provide leadership for these groups there are various kinds and diverse styles of leadership. Three basic kinds of leadership can be defined:

Appointed
Elected
Natural

The appointed leader is one who is given the assignment of functioning as leader by someone outside of the group. The leadership role in this case is usually clearly defined, its effectiveness depending on the skill of the appointed leader, the makeup of the group, and the willingness of the group to have that appointed leader. A second kind of leader is the elected leader. Here the group, either formally or semiformally, chooses someone from within the group, or occasionally from outside, to function as the leader for the group. The third and most powerful kind of leader in a small group is the natural leader. This is the person whom the group informally, often unconsciously, selects as a leader. It is usually someone who, sometimes unconsciously, assumes a leadership position within the group because of natural abilities demonstrated for leading that particular group, rather than by appointment or election. When the appointed or elected leader is also the natural leader, the leadership function will go rather smoothly. However, when the natural leader is some other member of the group, the leadership function begins to experience difficulty that will often surface in a power struggle between the natural leader and the appointed or elected leader.

Notice that we have not mentioned leaderless groups in this discussion. Leaderless groups have been very popular in some of the counseling, growth, study, and task-oriented groups. In a leaderless group no one is appointed or elected as the leader, and the group has the responsibility of leading itself, presumably through shared or rotating leadership. Yet, from the standpoint of our discussion here, there is really no such thing as a leaderless group; for in such groups the natural leader will emerge and take on the leadership function, although perhaps in a very quiet, "laid back" group-centered manner.

Five leadership styles can be identified. They are:

Technical expert
Authoritarian
Participatory
Group-centered
Facilitator

The technical expert is the leader who presumably has information or skill that the others in the group are lacking, at least to the same degree.[2] Expertise is then offered by the group leader to the other group members for their information and guidance. Typical of this kind of leadership is a teacher in a classroom. An authoritarian leader assumes the leadership role by virtue of the position that leader has in the organization or group, and uses that position of authority to justify and substantiate leadership. An example of this is the president of a corporation who assumes the role of designated authority and leadership with the company's executive committee. Participatory leadership is exercised by a leader, who while perhaps having an authority or technical expert position, chooses, once the group begins, to be a participant as well as a leader. This allows the leadership functions and information resources to move from person to person within the group. For example, the chairman of a department in a college may choose to use this style when meeting with colleagues in the department. Group-centered leadership comes close to what was referred to earlier as leaderless. Here the group as a whole assumes the leadership function. Again, the leadership func-

[2] As labeled by Yalom, *The Theory and Practice of Group Psychotherapy*, p. 110.

tion moves around the group with decisions made, usually by a strict adherence to total group concensus. A "pure" democracy functions in this way. The facilitator style of leadership is one in which the primary leadership function is to initiate the group session and to maintain a minimal amount of control over the direction the group takes, only as is necessary to keep the group on course toward the achievement of its goal or purpose.

The selection of the kind of leadership and the particular style to be used with a group depends on both the kind of group and its primary purposes and goals. When a new group is formed, and during the evaluation process, care should be taken in deciding which style and which kind of leadership best serves the group's needs. Incidentally, style of leadership may even need to change within the life of the group, depending again upon the group's purpose.

AN OVERVIEW OF THE SMALL GROUP PROCESS

The Nuts and Bolts: General Concerns

Purpose. Several group mechanics issues need to be answered as the group begins. These are the basic "whats" of the group's life. The first and most fundamental concern, the concern to which the leader and the group will return again and again throughout the life of the group is: What is the purpose of the group? It is extremely important to give a clear, concise, realistic, workable, and desirable definition of the purpose for the group. The more clearly the purpose is defined, the more realistic it is (many groups suffer from an unrealistic, grandiose statement of purpose); and the more desirable it is both to the leader and to the participants, the more likely the group will be experienced as productive and pleasurable, worthy of the members' investment of time and energy and, in some situations, money. An overall purpose for the group needs to be clearly defined, along with a brief statement of purpose for each major phase of the group's life.

Within that definition, the kind of group it is to be and the style of leadership to be given needs to be clearly stated. This definition will give direction to the formation of the group, its implementation, and the evaluation of the group's effectiveness.

Size. A second issue that needs to be considered as a group is formed is that of size. How many people should be included? This, of course, depends on the statement of purpose. Some groups, for example, educationally or socially oriented groups, can be quite large and still function very effectively. Therapy groups, on the other hand, tend to diminish in effectiveness when more than twelve people participate. Groups can be either too small or too large. An effectively functioning group requires a certain minimum number, a "critical mass," in order for it to be effective. Irwin Yalom's research suggests seven, with a range of from five to ten members, as an ideal number for counseling and psychotherapy groups,[3] while Bormann and Bormann suggest that seven or nine is ideal for task-oriented groups.[4] The larger the group is, the greater the tendency to naturally divide into subgroups.

Time. Another basic consideration is that of time. How many sessions should the group meet for, how frequently, and for how long each time? Again, a clear definition of the purpose of the group helps in determining the time frames for the group. Generally speaking, it seems to take three to six sessions of a group meeting weekly to "warm up" to each other so that the hard work of personal change, growth, and interpersonal depth can begin to occur. Yet, a task or educationally oriented group can have a useful life even after meeting for only a few sessions. The more change and growth oriented the group is, the longer the warm up takes. Most effective counseling, psychotherapy, and spiritual fellowship groups will meet regularly for up to two years. Beyond that,

[3] Yalom, *The Theory and Practice of Group Psychotherapy*, p. 254.
[4] Ernest Bormann and Nancy Bormann, *Effective Small Group Communication* (Minneapolis: Burgess, 1972), p. 6. In their research there is something about an odd number that is positively correlated to a group's effectiveness.

apathy or staleness sets in unless the purpose is redefined or the group begins the third stage of a group's life (we will discuss the stages of a small group shortly). For a group to develop and mold itself as an effectively functioning small group, some regularity of meeting is required with a minimum of every two weeks. A group that meets monthly has difficulty accomplishing much other than a task or organizational business and may be hampered in that task by never completing the first stage of a group's life. A group meeting less frequently than every two weeks is almost a new group each time it meets.

Some groups are open-ended, with no fixed terminating period. There are instances where the group members agree to meet together indefinitely until they choose to end the group. Other groups allow people to come and go as they please. Depending again upon the purpose of the group, groups that contract for meeting together for a specific length of time, with an openness to renegotiate the length as the group goes on, are preferred. It takes a few weeks to enfold new group members; when a group deifts on with no defined ending, there is usually no clear, clean closure for the individual or for the group. Yet, of course, that kind of openness may be important to the purpose of some groups. In any case, it is useful at the beginning of a group's life to clarify the duration of the group and how the group or the individuals will terminate. "Dropouts" without notice have a negative, demoralizing effect on a group. Remember, interpersonal trust usually develops only after a group has been together weekly for three to six sessions.

Typically, a group session is most effective when it meets for one and a half to two hours. It takes some time each session to begin working (ten to fifteen minutes or more, in some instances). After two hours, two dynamics often occur. First, when people know they have a long time in which to accomplish a task, they have a strong tendency to delay beginning work on that task, or to begin slowly. At the other end of the time frame, after two hours people get either restless or lethargic and little is effectively accomplished. Even in organizational meetings, it is my experience that little or no additional business can be accomplished after two hours. Growth and psychotherapy groups have experimented with marathons (eight to twenty-four hour sessions with breaks only for meals) and found them effective; thus they are used occasionally. Typically, however, an interpersonal group is most effective when it meets for one and a half to two hours, on a weekly or twice weekly schedule.

Physical Setting.   The physical space in which the group meets is another important consideration. It is important that the space be comfortable, but not too comfortable, and in keeping with the purpose of the group. Hard chairs at a table or desk, with bright lights, may be conducive to a task, business, or study oriented group, but not to a social, fellowship, support, or therapy group. Soft lounge chairs, irregularly arranged in a large room, with very soft light, is too comfortable for a growth, support, or therapy group; for it suggests rest rather than work. Therefore, a comfortable setting in a room of appropriate size, with good but not harsh lighting, and a physical arrangement in which there are no visual or auditory distractions is advisable. A study or growth group meeting in front of a large picture window looking out on the sights and sounds of a very active school playground will struggle to involve the participants in the work of the group, especially if the participants' children are on the playground. Furthermore, everyone should be within good eye contact range of each other, especially the leader, and there should be no unnecessary physical objects between the members of the group. People should be seated in a circular fashion at a comfortably close distance from one another; so that people can readily hear as well as see each other and feel the presence of the other participants.

Selection of Participants.   Potential participants are also determined by the purpose of the group. Often, in an effort to get "warm bodies" to fill up spaces in a group, people are recruited whose needs and interests, other than the universal need to belong, do not seem to fit that group. Therefore, care should be given to participant selection and inclusion. Generally, the ideal group member is someone who is verbal and has good social skills. On the other hand, people who are severely depressed, those who are prone to violence and have little impulse control, the actively psychotic, or the severely learning disabled usually do not function well in groups. That leaves the vast majority of the population as people who can receive from and contribute considerably to a small group.

The kind and style of leadership chosen also depends on the purpose and goal of the group. The particular leadership approach should be carefully chosen, as should the leader. The leader sets the boundaries, norm, and tone for the group and also models ideal group behavior. Keep in mind that the longer the group meets, the more the natural leader within the group will emerge.

Group norms or rules can be informal and remain undefined, or they can be clearly stated. It is my experience that a few simple, clearly stated norms help facilitate the group process. For some groups, a simple group contract that is verbally agreed to or actually signed facilitates the healthy, energetic development of the group. With a clear contract, members can agree to the expectations and procedures of the group.[5]

The Dynamics Involved in an Effective Group

As a leader, it is very helpful to be able to focus one's attention on the process and the dynamics of the group more than on the content of the group, particularly if the group has a growth, support, fellowship, or therapeutic orientation, as compared to a task or educational purpose. The skilled leader needs to be able to track the group on two levels simultaneously: the content level, to make sure it flows, and the process level, with a concern toward what helps facilitate and what interferes with the effectiveness of the group. Involved

[5] Sample group contracts and covenants are included in the appendix.

with this processing is the need for the leader, and often for the entire group, to periodically evaluate the progress of the group.

The key ingredients for an effective group are the following: commitment, cohesiveness, clarity, communication. Being able to communicate effectively, using the tools and procedures of good communication, including clarity of subject matter and interpersonal communication, is crucial to an effective, productive, satisfying group. Group cohesiveness, all the forces holding the members together, is necessary for them to remain together as a group. And, throughout the group's life, the commitment of the participants to the group, its purpose, process, and people, will significantly effect the value and outcome of the group experience.

Ten "curative factors" of psychotherapy groups are listed by Irwin Yalom of Stanford University in his text, *The Theory and Practice of Group Psychotherapy* (1970, 1975). These are the ten group dynamics that research has found to be the most helpful ingredients in group effectiveness. They are positively correlated to client results. They are the ten dynamics that are important to the vitality of nearly any small group, whether a therapy group or a study group, and they have general as well as particular application. These factors, these primary dynamics, are as follows:

> Imparting of information
> Instillation of hope
> Universality
> Altruism
> Recapitulation of primary family
> Development of socializing techniques
> Interpersonal learning
> Group cohesiveness
> Imitative behavior
> Catharsis

Each of these factors and other significant dynamics will be discussed in some detail in the succeeding chapters, identifying and describing the dynamics that are important to each stage of the group's development.

Gerard Egan of Loyola University has written an extremely
helpful manual for training effective counselors, entitled *The
Skilled Helper* (Monterey, Calif.: Brooks/Cole, 1975). Building
from Roger's therapeutic triad (unconstitutional positive regard, accurate empathy, and congruence) and the works of
Carkhuff, Truax, and others who have been involved in a systematic skill development approach to training counselors and
therapists, Egan lists twelve counseling skills important to the
effectiveness of the helping process. They are:

Attending
Primary accurate empathy
Respect (unconditional positive regard)
Genuineness (congruence)
Concreteness
Advanced accurate empathy
Immediacy
Confrontation
Alternative frames of reference
Self-disclosure
Elaboration of action programs, including goal setting
Support

These counselor, or helper, skills are the same basic skills
needed for the skilled group leader, particularly one who desires that the group be meaningful and helpful for every participant. Each of these helping and leadership skills will be
discussed in the chapters that follow, placing them within a
developmental framework and indicating which skills are particularly important in a particular stage of the group's life.

While the above list is somewhat lengthy and can appear
to be overwhelming at first glance, Egan indicates that these
skills are not overly sophisticated and difficult, requiring years
and years of graduate study. Rather, they are, he emphasizes,
basic human relations skills, reflected in people who are highly
effective in their interpersonal relationships. They are, in
short, friendship skills. While profound and requiring hard

19

work in their implementation, these skills are simple, nonacademic, nonesoteric skills. A skilled leader is simply an effectively living person who cares (skillfully, through accurate empathy and respect), is genuine, speaks concretely, is willing to confront, and focuses on practical action. Stated another way, a competent, skilled, small group leader is:

> Caring
> Confronting
> Congruent
> Concrete

A DEVELOPMENTAL APPROACH

As with individual counseling, we can observe four distinct stages in the development and life history of a small group. These stages are developmental stages. That is, each stage builds on and includes the previous stage. Furthermore, each stage requires the sufficient, though not necessarily total, completion of the previous stage in order for the group to function at the current stage. In addition, there are particular group dynamics operative at each stage, with certain leadership skills that are important to each. The individual counseling relationship builds through three developmental stages for Egan, with three distinctive goals for the helper and three related goals for the counselees. The client's goals are as follows for Egan: Stage I—Self-Exploration; Stage II—Dynamic Self-Understanding; Stage III—Acting. In the overview that follows, these client goals are adapted to group goals through the four stages of a group's life. The helper goals Egan lists are: Pre-Helping; Attending; Stage I—Responding; Stage II—Integrative Understanding; Stage III—Facilitating Action.[6] These developmental helper goals have also been adapted to our understanding of group leadership. In addition to Egan's three stages, there is a fourth developmental stage which is an important, although often neglected stage; that is *termination*. Nearly ev-

---

[6] Gerard Egan, *The Skilled Helper* (Monterey, Calif., Brooks/Cole Division of Wadsworth Publishing Co., Inc., 1975), p. 30.

ery group experiences this stage, yet rarely is it recognized in its place in the overall group experience.

While all of the group dynamics are potentially present at each stage, and each leadership skill is important to all stages, there are particular dynamics and skills crucial to a particular stage. While new dynamics and skills come into focus at each stage, a developmental approach affirms the assumption that there is a cumulative factor. That is to say, at Stage II the dynamics and leadership skills of Stage I are concurrently present with all the new dynamics and leadership skills of Stage II. Likewise, in Stages III and IV all of the dynamics and leadership skills of both Stages I and II are present, along with those added by Stage III.

Another important factor in taking a developmental approach to the life of a small group is to recognize the goal orientation of the small group. A goal is defined not only as an overall megagoal for the group's life, but also as minigoals for each stage of a group's development. This recognizes that certain goals are possible at certain points in the group's life, and that to try to accomplish effective personal action without having first accomplished inclusion, understanding, and personal growth, is unrealistic. Furthermore, it suggests that we start with the overall goal, define it in terms of some concrete action, and then work back, thinking of a sequence of ingredients that would enable the group to get to that point. The question to be asked repeatedly in forming appropriate minigoals is: What has to be learned and accomplished before the desired action can take place?

Within this goal orientation it is important not only for the group to have clearly defined goals, but also to recognize that the leader needs to define leadership goals for each stage as well. The effective group leader should be aware of any conflict or similarity between the leader's goals and the individual participant's goals. As we shall discuss later, the more collaborative and the more parallel the goals are at each stage, the more shared participation in and commitment to the group is likely to characterize the group's experience. It is also useful to distinguish between primary and secondary goals with a utilization of the KIS principle (Keep It Simple!). Per-

Table 1 An Overview

	Stage I	Stage II	Stage III	Stage IV
Group Goals	Inclusion Self/subject exploration	Work—growth Self/subject understanding	Action Support Evaluation	Termination
Group Dynamics	Housekeeping Details: 1) Definition of purpose 2) Logistics of time, space, etc. 3) Selection of leadership, kind and style 4) Membership composition 5) Contract or covenant; rules and norms Providing information Socializing Genuine concern Common experience Emotional expression Informal formation of rules and norms An atmosphere of hope	Cohesiveness Creation of family Learning from each other Imitating the leader Transition and change Evaluation	Cooperation Subgrouping Conflict Risk-taking Action-taking Reflection, evaluation, and reinforcement	Termination
Leader Goals	Responding Leading	Understanding Facilitating Integrating	Facilitate action Support Reinforcement Evaluate	Conclude
Leader Skills	Paying attention Communicating basic empathy Being genuine Being concrete Conveying respect Using effective communication Kindness	Advanced empathy Confrontation Leader disclosure Talking about us Articulating alternatives Encouragement	Facilitate Develop action programs Provide support Keep the focus of responsibility clear Evaluate Challenge[7]	Termination

[7] "Kindness," "Encouragement," "Challenge," are the three stages of love as described by Father John Powell in his book, *Unconditional Love* (Niles, Illinois: Argus, 1969), and used here as a summary of the leadership skills needed at each stage.

haps for most groups that are designed to effect the growth and development of each participant, the goal or process is to move from a leader–recipient participant to a leader–participant sharing ("collaborative"), to the participant becoming a leader in that or another group.

With that goal in mind, we begin now to examine each of the stages of a group's life.

ACTIVE LEARNING EXERCISES FOR
CHAPTER ONE

Learning occurs best when the content that we receive rather passively through reading or listening can be actively practiced and experienced. Ideally, the concepts of small group leadership and dynamics can best be taught through a combination of content verbally presented, skills modeled by a highly competent group leader, and the active practice of leadership skills with feedback from others. Whether or not you have the opportunity to observe the leadership skills discussed in these pages modeled by a highly skilled leader, active learning exercises are included at the conclusion of each chapter. These exercises are designed to give you an opportunity to practice the small group leadership skills in a learning group, thus encouraging a more complete awareness of the dynamics of the skills discussed in this book.

The active learning exercises will be most effective if they are used in a small learning group of six to eight people that meet together in the same group throughout the learning experience, with each person having the opportunity to function as a practice leader at least once every chapter. The others will, in addition to being participants in a practice group, observe the group dynamics that are operative and provide feedback to the practice leader. Furthermore, while role-playing hypothetical situations is useful, the more personal and authentic the material presented in the learning experience is, the more effective the practice will be.

Here, then, are the active learning exercises for Chapter One.

(1) Select one member of the practice group as the leader, with the others as participants. Briefly note what kind of group and what kind of leader is desired for this practice group.

(2) Have each participant describe the small groups that might exist at work, in an organization, and so on. Assess together what kinds of groups these might be and what kinds and styles of leadership are exercised, as well as what developmental stages the groups go through.

(3) Have each participant describe one negative and one positive small group experience from the past, telling the value of the positive group experience and what seemed to be common to the two group experiences.

(4) Observe the beginning "nuts and bolts" of this practice group. How do setting, time of day, duration, size, implicit or explicit goal, contract and/or norms, facilitate or hinder the group process? Negotiate together any changes that the group wants to make in these details.

(5) Have each person discuss what he or she is feeling, thinking, and/or wanting for the practice group.

Stage I—Inclusion and Exploration

Having answered the preliminary questions, such as the purpose of the group, its size, the style of leadership desired, its duration and norms, the small group is ready to begin. As we have indicated, a small group, given enough time and leadership skill, will go through three distinct developmental stages in the life of that group. The first is the most crucial stage. It is the stage of inclusion and exploration. These are the tasks and the goals of the beginning of a group's life.

GROUP DYNAMICS—STAGE ONE

Group Goals

The primary initial goal of a group is to include each of the participants. The beginning group requires the discovery and utilization of the means by which members of that group will feel included within the group. Each group paticipant needs to believe that participation in the group is important, not only to oneself, but also to the group as a whole. In order for the participants to give themselves to the group process long enough and with enough investment of emotional energies for the group to be beneficial to them, they must feel as if they belong. There is little motivation for continuing participation in a group for a person who feels excluded. According to Maslow's "hierarchy of needs," the participants' belonging needs have to be met before they are able to explore, discover, grow, and ultimately take constructive action based on the group experience, thereby satisfying esteem and self-actualization needs.[1]

At the same time, if the group participants are going to perceive the group to be worthwhile, they must develop an attitude or stance of exploration. Depending upon the purpose of the group, that eagerness or willingness to explore might be focused on self-exploration or exploring the content or dynamics of a particular topic. The people who are involved in the group will need, in the beginning phase of the life of that group, or at the start of their membership in the group, a willingness to explore their knowledge, beliefs, relationships, emotions, behavior, task, or the subject matter around which the group is formed. It is necessary that a person in a group believe that participation in the group is going to be beneficial in some way; that it will lead to new insight, behavior, feelings, beliefs, achievements, and so on. To do that, the participant in a group must be willing to explore, investigate, and thus to participate actively.

The primary functions of the group's leadership, therefore, are helping to include the participants and leading them into exploration. The primary tool the leader has, in Powell's sequence of love, is kindness. It is the leader who demonstrates and expresses kindness and caring and who conveys to group members their importance to the group and the group's importance to them. It is through kindness that a partici- will feel secure and comfortable, and thus be able and lling to explore new thoughts, feelings, convictions, and actions.

[1] See Abraham Maslow, *Motivation and Personality*, rev. ed. (New York: Harper & Row, 1970), pp. 35–38, for a description of the "hierarchy of needs."

During Stage I, the leader also helps to establish the style of the group's life through listening, responding, and leading. In this process, the leader models appropriate or desired group behavior and establishes its norms in practice as well as in words. By listening, responding, and leading, the leader helps to encourage the experience of inclusion and the willingness to explore on the part of the group member.

Helpful Group Dynamics

When the group has had its first session, and through the next several sessions, particular dynamics are important in establishing the effectiveness of that group. While there is no absolute order in which these dynamics come into operation, they are discussed below in their approximate sequence. These critical and helpful Stage I group dynamics are housekeeping details, providing important information, socializing, genuine concern or altruism, common experience, emotional expression, the informal formation of rules and norms, and the development of an atmosphere of hope.

Housekeeping Details. In the first chapter we discussed the "nuts and bolts" or housekeeping issues involved in the formation of the group. While most of these details are decided upon and communicated to potential members before the first group session, they are part of the initial dynamics in the first stage of a group's life. They are also present throughout the group's life, as part of the group's formal or informal contract, and as housekeeping details are occasionally discussed and adjusted. Yet, participants often come to the first session with only a vague understanding of the purpose of the group, confusion or uncertainty over some of the logistical details, limited awareness of the leadership style chosen, curiosity and/or apprehension in regard to the other participants, and varied understanding and acceptance of the formal or informal contract, rules, and norms. A restatement and clarification of the purpose of the group at the first session is important. This purpose may need to be restated or reaffirmed several times over the life of the group. It is the overall goal and purpose of the group that helps focus and direct the group session after session.

The logistics of time, space, and so on, need to be restated at the beginning. Often there are necessary or desirable adjustments in meeting time, location, physical arrangement, and accoutrements that are required to facilitate the group's effectiveness. A clear definition of the kind and style of leadership selected for the group is important to the first meeting(s). Sometimes adjustments in leadership style are indicated after the group has formed. Leadership kind and style are selected to serve the purpose and goal of the group; therefore, they are flexible and responsive to the participants and their resources. Early in the group's life the membership composition may change—one person may leave, and one or more may join. Or, if the group is established for a particular task, a change in membership may be required for the accomplishment of the particular task. Clarification and adjustment in the contract, covenant, rules, or norms will need to be made based on the needs and interests of the altered group.

Throughout this first stage, it is important to maintain a healthy balance between solid, secure structure and flexibility to the particular circumstances. Housekeeping, setting up the basic ordering of the group's life, is an important dynamic as the group is launched. Order, efficiency, and goal orientation are important ingredients in helping participants to feel included and begin the adventure of self or subject exploration.

Providing Information.   Providing information is important in order for the group to be effective, especially during the initial stage. The leader or other group member giving a new member important information concerning the group itself—its purpose, ground rules or norms, expectations, and/ or other group housekeeping details—can foster a feeling of importance and inclusion in the group's life. Basic information can also provide a sense of the structure of the group, which helps to alleviate the fear of the unknown or fear of wasted time and effort. Through this basic information, the participant will know that the group has limitations and parameters that both enable it to progress and make the progression safe. This seems to be particularly important when new participants have some fear of the small group based on the reputation of small groups generally, or of this group particularly. This is providing information or content *about* the group.

In addition, it may be useful to convey something about the content of the group, that is, the subject matter on which the group will be focusing. That is to say, early in the group's life there is value in a direct educational approach that conveys data about the group's subject matter. At this early phase of the group's life, teaching about the specific content of the group is useful in establishing an atmosphere of inclusion and in stimulating exploration. This teaching often functions as an initial binding force for the group, pulling it together with common information.

Yet, in developing an effective future for the group, great caution must be exercised while providing this information. Information presented in an authoritarian or advising manner will be counterproductive. A leader who exercises a heavy hand at the beginning of a group encourages the development of protectiveness or defensiveness that leaves the participant closed rather than open. The data that is presented should be given enthusiastically, eagerly, yet in an open manner, inviting participation by the others. In order to be most effective, it should be directed toward stimulating exploration rather than toward providing final answers.

Socializing.   Social learning is another important factor at Stage I. The socializing process occurs in all groups as people learn appropriate or desired behaviors through socializing with others, observing the socializing patterns and strategies going on among other members of the group, and imitating the socializing skills of the group's leader. It is the nature of groups, whether for good or evil, that group participants tend to accept the values and norms of that group. This certainly can be and has been used to lead people into inappropriate and ineffective behaviors, values, and attitudes; yet it can also be used positively to effect healthier behaviors, beliefs, feelings, and so on, that are more in keeping with the individual's well-being and growth as a person. This socializing impact can be used in a manipulative manner, or simply as a fact of life about peoples' participation in groups.

The socializing process in a group provides opportunity for accurate interpersonal feedback for the participant. The group member can observe how her or his behavior effects other people, and hear the others describe their thoughts, feelings, and intentions in response to that behavior.

The socializing process is also important as a source of the enjoyment that comes from participating in and perceiving the value of the group. When socializing is good, people have more fun, and the group builds greater trust, cohesiveness, interest, enthusiasm, and commitment to the group.

Good Will—Genuine Concern. A fourth potent ingredient in a beginning group is the expression or experience of altruism, that is, respect, caring, mutual regard, warmth, and love. While it is certainly important coming from the leader or facilitator of the group, mutual regard coming from other members of the group is especially powerful in conveying inclusion and, eventually, in effecting change and growth in a participant, or producing the motivation to accomplish a group task. Having people who care for and help each other is one of the most basic and important needs of every person. When received, it stimulates our development. Reflecting and modeling a high level of respect and warmth (what Rogers and others called "unconditional positive regard"), is crucial to effective leadership. Indeed, the leader will often create an atmosphere of caring that other group members will tend to copy; and in a sense they, too, are expected to care, as part of their role in the group. When deep caring is expressed by other members of the group, more dynamics, more energy, and more impact result. This increases the value of the group to the individual participant, both in terms of enjoyment and participation in the group and in its benefit to him.

In a group characterized by a high level of altruism, there are many relationship bonds that are formed, and leadership is often shared. One of the most potent ways of helping someone is to let them help you; thus when there is mutual regard within an effectively functioning group, there are numerous opportunities for a participant to be a helper as well as a "helpee." It is important to treat all ideas, opinions, feelings, and convictions as valid and worth sharing in order to encourage an atmosphere of mutual caring.

Common Experience. A fifth helping dynamic in Stage I of the small group process is common experience, or the experience of universality. Universality is what Yalom calls "the disconfirmation of feelings of uniqueness."[2] This is the discovery that you are not alone and unique, but that others have had similar experiences, thoughts, feelings, and concerns. The group is especially powerful in conveying that experience to its participants. In a lecture, in a one-on-one relationship, or in reading, that awareness of universality can be discovered; however, the experience is not the same as when someone else in a group reveals something about himself or herself and one or more affirm that they too have experienced something very similar. What was theoretical truth in other settings suddenly becomes existential truth within the context of the group.

There is, in this experience of universality, a sense that we are all connected to each other as part of the human family who share the human condition. We are all human and we all struggle. All of us put our pants on one leg at a time. We do have a common bond of humanness with all others. With this experience, the realization comes that someone else understands and can empathize with us. We are not alone, weird, or vastly different. That discovery is very freeing to a person who thought that he or she alone had that problem, that fear, that excitement, that belief, that doubt, or that unusual experience. We are in this thing together, and there is comfort, relief, strength, and hope in that awareness.

Emotional Expression. Another important ingredient at this first stage of a group's life is the opportunity for catharsis. To be able to express emotion in an open, nondestructive

---

[2] Yalom, *The Theory and Practice of Group Psychotherapy*, pp. 7–9.

way, whatever that emotion may be, is important for both the group and the individual participant. The kind and the amount of emotional release that is appropriate is to some degree related to the purpose of the group (e.g., there is a difference between a task oriented group and a therapy group as to the amount of emotional release that is helpful or hindering to the group's accomplishment of its purposes). The more personal growth oriented the group is, the more important is catharsis. Often, intense emotions need to be released before there can be an openness that allows and encourages people to move ahead. Even in organizational or task groups, the freedom for emotional response is important for the group's progress, as well as for the individuals involved. Sometimes groups organized around tasks or organizational leadership can become stuck because of intense emotions that exist in one or more of the individuals within the group. If these emotions were expressed openly, the group could move on to other issues more freely.

A caution is important here. Except for groups that exist for the sole or primary purpose of releasing pent-up emotions, catharsis should not happen too soon nor too frequently. Neither should the release of emotion be the primary focus. It is an ingredient in the group process and not the entire process. Tears, the open expression, anger, frustration, fondness, warmth, and fear need to be gently encouraged, not forced nor artificially manufactured, and gently controlled or kept within limits of appropriateness and usefulness. Allowing or encouraging catharsis is another way of conveying respect, warmth, and caring.

Informal Formation of Rules and Norms. While it is very useful for a group to have established rules and norms for the structuring and guiding of the group's life (indicating appropriate and useful facilitative behaviors), many informal, undefined rules and norms are formed in the early development of the group. This is the beginning of the formation of the family system discussed in Chapter 3 as a Stage II dynamic. Certain ways of relating and behaving are repeated by individuals within a group; thus a definite pattern develops.

Various roles or housekeeping chores are assumed by particular people, and certain rituals are unconsciously reenacted by members of the group, evolving into informal, usually undiagnosed and undefined rules and norms. These develop rather quickly and spontaneously. The skilled group leader will understand that this is inevitable and be sensitive to and develop an awareness of these informal norms.

An Atmosphere of Hope.   Finally, the creation of an atmosphere of hope is important to this first stage in a group's life. Participants need to believe that the group experience will be valuable to them. The group member's faith that the time spent will be effective and/or enjoyable will make a significant contribution to the impact of the group for that person. If participants are hopeful, they will enter into the life of the group enthusiastically and energetically, and they will behave more genuinely within the group; thus increasing the transferability of the group experience to their daily experience outside the group.

Furthermore, expectations are closely correlated to results. Numerous psychological experiments have demonstrated this correlation. For example, one group of Harvard graduate students was told that a population of laboratory mice were "maze bright"; they could learn a maze pattern factor faster than a cross-section of mice. Another group of students were given mice who were labeled "maze dull"; it took these mice greater time to accomplish the maze than the average. While both populations of mice were essentially the same, those mice labeled "maze bright" did, in fact, learn the maze faster. The expectations of the graduate students made a difference in the speed at which the mice learned the maze. Hope was transferred from the experimenters to the mice with positive results. Another experiment emphasizing the powerful impact of the instillation of positive expectations, in this case hope. was a research project with teachers in the San Francisco Public School System. Groups of students were tested on standard intelligence tests and divided into two nearly identical groups. One group of students was placed with teachers who were told that these students were exceptional, bright, eager students; the other group was placed with teachers who were told that these students were not highly motivated nor did they possess superior intelligence. After several weeks, both groups of students were tested with the same instrument. The result was that students who were expected to perform at high levels scored higher at the conclusion of the experiment than those who were not expected to perform well. The hope of a teacher for his or her students made a positive impact on the performance of those students.[3] Thus, the instillation of hope, that is, the expectation of positive results of a group experience, does have an impact on the eventual effectiveness of that group.

Therefore, within limits of appropriateness and balance with other factors, whatever the leader and the other group members can do to realistically build hope in the value or helpfulness of the group experience for each participant, should be encouraged. This will make a significant difference for the usefulness of the group to the participant. The occasional use of success stories or testimonials of other groups is one useful device. However, it must be understood that these stories and other expressions of enthusiasm and hope are to be used for encouraging the current participants, rather than to prove a point.

LEADERSHIP FUNCTIONS AND SKILLS AT STAGE I

Leadership Goals

We move now to the leadership functions and skills that are important to this first stage of a small group. As we have already indicated, the primary goal of Stage I is to enable the group participants to feel included and to believe that they are important to the life of the group. That is to say, they

[3] Robert Rosenthal, *Experimenter Effects in Behavior Research* (New York: Halsted Press, Division of John Wiley & Sons, 1976).

have a place, they belong; the group is perceived as being "for" them. Working with the foundation of inclusion, the participant can begin the process of exploration and discovery. Thus, the group leader's objective at this first stage is to facilitate a sense of belonging and a readiness to explore. The leader does this through kindness, through responding eagerly and frequently to each group member, and through establishing the life of the group by exercising leadership. A measurable goal for the leader at this point is the enabling of group members to get involved to the point of wanting to return for and freely participate in the succeeding sessions. Usually, if a person has returned for the second, third, and fourth sessions, that participant will continue through phase one and be ready to move into phase two.

Leadership Skills

Paying Attention.   The first skill at Stage I is that of paying attention (what Egan calls "attending"). Egan lists four ingredients in active attending: social intelligence, physical presence, psychological presence, and minimal encouragements to talk.[4]

An effective small group leader has good social awareness and skills—that is, social intelligence. Stated in another way, the effective leader is comfortable with people and has the capacity to understand them—to hear what they are saying, observe what they are doing, and know something about what that behavior means for those people; furthermore, they are able to communicate that awareness to others clearly and directly. A person with good social intelligence is able to act— to translate perceptions and ideas into actions and to integrate discrimination with communication and other forms of activity. The leader is able to act on the basis of her or his thinking. Awareness of oneself and others leads a socially intelligent person to action.

[4] Egan, *The Skilled Helper,* pp. 55–72.

A leader demonstrates good social intelligence, good "attending," through being physically present with the members of the group. "Attending" requires an intensity of presence, a sense of being "with" the other person. Physically, the effective leader does that by first removing anything that might distract him or her from paying full attention to each of the members of the group, within limits of appropriateness and reasonableness. For example, a noisy television or stereo would be turned off, or a door to a busy hallway closed. The physical surroundings, as noted earlier, need to be comfortable, but not too comfortable, and free from distractions. Furthermore, there should be no objects between the leader and the group members except those which are necessary or useful for the purpose of a group. People need to be situated so that there is ready eye contact between each member of the small group.

Egan's description of the posture of "attending" or involvement can be summarized with the acrostic SOLER.[5] The leader assumes a posture of facing the other person *s*quarely and directly. The leader adopts an *o*pen posture, with a slight *l*ean toward the person to whom attention is directed at that moment. The leader has good *e*ye contact with the group member, and all of these physical actions should be expressed with a *r*elaxed and natural posture. Rigid, overly aggressive or assertive "attending" can be counterproductive and discouraging to the group participant. So too, overly casual or timid "attending" may convey to the group member a feeling of unimportance and/or that the group experience is not really that significant. The effective group leader is physically active and is perceived as warm, friendly, outgoing, encouraging and respectful.

Psychological "attending" is conveyed primarily through listening. We feel included by another when we believe that we are being actively listened to. When someone conveys that what we say is being paid close attention to, we feel important and think that our verbal participation with that person is respected. Thus, we are encouraged to continue in the group and to explore ourselves or the subject matter

[5] Egan, *The Skilled Helper,* p. 65.

in relation to the purpose of the group. Our nonverbal behaviors—facial expressions, body language (the use or nonuse of SOLER), and paralinguistic behaviors (our manner of speaking: tone of voice, rate of speech, inflection, and pitch) all reflect the intensity of our listening, and therefore our interest in what is being said. How often have you been discouraged in continuing a conversation because the person you were talking with was looking around and away from you while you were talking, or was walking back and forth with folded arms, holding a tightly clenched jaw, continually peering at his or her watch, or grunting unenthusiastic responses to what you were saying? An effective listener listens intently not only to the actual content of what a person is saying, but also for feelings and meanings. The context of what is being said is important along with the content; yet it is important for the skillful listener to have actively heard the content first.[6]

Finally, there are responses that a listener can make that are minimal, yet helpful, encouragements to talk. Simple responses such as "Uh-huh," "Yeah," "Really?", "Tell me more," "Keep going," are behavioral responses that let the other person know you are listening and that you care. Thus they are encouraged to continue talking. As they participate (within reasonable limits, for each person in a group needs to be heard and thus included), they feel included and are more likely to be eager to participate, explore, discover, and move on to Stage II. "Attending" is a simple, basic social skill.

Basic Empathy—Explicit Content. This second leadership function, while simple and basic, requires more effort and skillfulness. Egan describes this helping or leadership skill as primary accurate empathy. Most people with human relations education are aware of empathy (the capacity of being "with" another person and of understanding that person) and

---

[6] We will not discuss active listening skills at this point for there are outstanding resources (books, courses, etc.) that teach listening skills. Two particularly helpful resources are *Talking Together I* (Minneapolis: Interpersonal Communication Programs, Inc., 1979, by Miller, Nunnally, and Wackman); and chapters three and four, entitled "How to Listen So Kids Will Talk to You," and "Putting Your Active Listening Skills to Work," in Thomas Gordon's *Parent Effectiveness Training* (New York: New American Library, Plume Books, 1975).

its importance in helping people. It is also important as a basic skill to be employed in developing good interpersonal relationships. Rogers listed accurate empathy as one of the ingredients in the therapeutic triad.[7] Other researchers in psychotherapy have also emphasized that empathy is a crucial factor for people being helped through a relationship with another person.

Egan differentiates between primary and secondary levels of accurate empathy. Primary accurate empathy is the accurate discrimination or understanding of the content of what a person is saying; what they have said has been accurately understood as to content and any of the life context (the life situation or feelings of the individual) that was revealed by or explicit in the content (for example, "I'm uptight . . ." "I'm thrilled . . ." "Being out of work is scary," and, "It's great to be alive on a warm spring day!"). Secondary, or advanced, accurate empathy responds to and discriminates the internal context and implied meanings. This advanced level of empathy is essentially a Stage II leadership skill and is discussed there at greater length. In this first stage, basic accurate empathy is a vital ingredient in the leadership skills of the small group leader.

Importance of Accuracy. It is vitally important that empathy be accurate for it to be helpful in encouraging inclusion and exploration. A group member's message needs to be understood from within that person's frame of reference or experience—that is, that the leader understand the participant's message, what it means, and what it feels like to the participant. It is essential that the leader's accurate understanding be communicated to the participant. A simple paraphrase of what the person says is usually the most effective. If the message sender believes the leader has accurately heard what has been said, that person will feel understood and included and will perhaps respond with a nod, a sigh, "Uh-hun," "Yeah," "That's it," "Eureka!" We all know how frustrating or discouraging it is to tell someone about something very important

    [7] C. R. Rogers, E. Gendlin, D. Kiesler and C. B. Truax, *The Therapeutic Relationship and Its Impact* (Madison, Wisconsin: University of Wisconsin Press, 1967).

to us, only to have them misinterpret what we have just said. It is even more annoying if they have coupled this misunderstanding with the phrase "I understand." Simply stated, basic primary level accurate empathy is good listening and accurate communication. The immediate goals of primary level accurate empathy are to establish rapport and to develop an atmosphere of trust and openness that encourages active participation by the group member.

Hindrances to Basic Empathy. There are several problems or hindrances that are common to the attempt to communicate accurate empathy, according to Egan.[8] The first is to simply say nothing, to fail to respond. A second common problem is that of distorting the content, that is, to be inaccurate in the empathic response through interpretation, through hearing or responding to only part of the message, or by adding to what was said. The goal of accurate empathy is to make certain that the message heard is the equivalent of the message sent and not more than, less than, or different from the original message. Another common problem is that of failing to respond to feelings conveyed in the giving of the message, not taking them into active consideration. A fourth problem in communicating empathy is to fake understanding, pretending to know. Perhaps nothing hinders the experience of empathy more than pretending to understand, except for direct criticism or judgment of the person for what has been said. A further hindrance to empathy is for the listener to jump in too quickly, not allowing the speaker to complete the thought or express the feeling he or she wants to communicate. The opposite can also be a problem. By allowing a person to go on and on and on, the message can be distorted or accurate understanding can be hindered. A sixth problem in communicating accurate empathy is the failure to use the language of the person one is listening to. Empathy, particularly at this first stage, needs to utilize the frame of reference of the speaker, particularly through utilizing their words.

Guidelines for Basic Empathy. Having listed the problems that interfere with the communication of accurate empa-

---

[8] Egan, *The Skilled Helper,* pp. 79–89.

thy, Egan lists eight rules for the use of "primary accurate empathy."[9] First, attend carefully—give the other your full attention, physically and psychologically. A second rule is to listen for the basic or core message that the person is communicating. While a person may be saying several things, there may be one basic thing that he or she is saying. Third, respond frequently, yet briefly and tentatively. It is useful to kindly interrupt a person, to respond to small, bite-sized portions, and not wait until the meal is concluded. It is very difficult to accurately respond to a long involved statement; rather, frequent responses convey your "attending" behavior and increase the accuracy of your empathic responses. Yet these responses need to be very brief and tentative. Remember, you, as the leader of a small group, are listening to them, not they to you (unless it is a group organized around the technical expert model and your task is to convey authority or expert information). In the end, the participant is the authority about the content of the message; therefore, the leader's empathic response should be tentative. A skilled leader does not tell the participant what he or she is saying. Instead, that leader accurately reflects what the participant is saying.

A fourth rule in communicating basic empathy is that of responding with gentleness and with strength. The skilled leader is kind in the communication of empathy, expressing that leader's regard and respect for the person with confidence and strength. Fifth, to be effective, the leader needs to respond to both the feelings and the content, utilizing the words that the person uses and/or documenting observations of that person's feelings. Sixth, a good leader moves gradually. Don't jump too quickly to conclusions or more abruptly through the conversation. Moreover, the leader needs to allow and encourage the message to be carefully and completely, though not exhaustively, conveyed. Another rule is that the leader pay careful attention to cues in regard to the accuracy of the emphatic response. If you have accurately understood a person and have communicated that understanding, that per-

[9] Egan, *The Skilled Helper*, p. 89.

son will usually give some behavioral sign that he or she has been understood, through a nod, a sigh of relief, or with words such as: "yes, that's it!" "yeah," and "really." Without that cue, the leader may want to briefly restate or ask the person to clarify the message. Finally, it is useful to note signs of stress reactions or resistance to the leader's response.

In summary, the guidelines for communicating basic accurate empathy are as follows:

1. Attend carefully.
2. Listen to basic or core messages.
3. Respond frequently, briefly, and tentatively.
4. Respond with gentleness and strength.
5. Respond to both feelings and content.
6. Do not jump to conclusions.
7. Pay attention to accuracy clues.
8. Note signs of stress or resistance.

Being Genuine. Genuineness is an additional crucial skill for the effective small group leader, especially at this initial stage of the group's life. It is important that the leader be perceived as a real, authentic person. Phonies, or people who appear to be phoney, discourage the building of rapport and trust which are critically important to helping the group member to feel included and to begin exploring. A more technical word for genuineness is congruence. A congruent person is the same on the outisde as on the inside, and thoughts, feelings, and behavior are consistent. What one says he or she feels or thinks, is what that person feels or thinks.

Genuineness is communicated through an avoidance of playing professional in the group, thus hiding oneself from the members of the group. A genuine person is spontaneous, natural, and free in behavior within the group. Nondefensiveness also characterizes a genuine person, as do openness to criticism, suggestions, and praise, and willingness to examine one's own behavior, thoughts, wants, and feelings. In that way, the leader of a small group is also a participant or member of that group. Furthermore, a genuine person exhibits a measure of consistency—being the same person in any setting. And finally, genuineness is reflected in self-sharing, a willingness to be identified with the members of the group and share beliefs, intentions, emotions, and so on.

Being Concrete. Another leadership skill that is vitally important at this initial stage in the group's life is (according to Carkhuff, Egan, and others) concreteness. This is the process whereby the leader, in communicating accurate empathy, the group's purpose and norms, genuineness, and respect states his or her response in a concise, precise, specific manner. Vague generalities are made specific and precise. Implicit messages are made explicit. Long, rambling statements are made concise. General problems become specific problems leading to specific solutions wherever possible. So much time and energy in a group can be lost by vague, generalized, undefined conversation. The more the conversation is focused on specific problems, concerns, issues, ideas, experiences, wants, and behaviors, the more included, hopeful, and encouraged to explore the members will feel. The group leader is the model for this behavior for the group. The more concrete the leader is, the more the group members will learn to be concrete.

One communication skill that can greatly enhance the development of concreteness is that of "speaking of self" or making "I statements." First person statements encourage concreteness. Second and third person statements discourage being focused and specific. Note the difference in concreteness between "Everyone is concerned about the economy today," and "I feel anxious and frustrated over the cost of gasoline each time I fill my car with gas."

Concreteness is further encouraged when conversation is focused on material related to the purpose or topic of the group and the group is not allowed to ramble from subject to subject. Asking for more specific information or for a clarification of a statement may encourage concreteness. Questions that ask "what," "when," "who," or "how" help make a conversation concrete, whereas "why" tends to make the conversation more vague, general, and defensive. Also, a focus on the present facilitates concreteness, while a focus on the past or distant future encourages a lack of concreteness in a group, except as such past or future material relates to the "here and now." There is greater personal risk in being concrete, both for the leader and for the group member; yet there is more potential for decision making, personal growth, and task accomplishment. If a group becomes boring to a member of the group or even to you as a leader, you may want to ask if the interactions are concrete.

Conveying Respect for the Participant. Another critical skill at this first stage is that of respect. In fact, it is a skill needed at each stage and in any form of helpful human encounter. Respect is equivalent to what has been called unconditional positive regard. More simply, it is warmth and comes close to an ancient meaning for love. Respect is something you genuinely have or do not have for the people with whom you are working. There are ways to convey to the members of your group your respect for them. Included are one's basic orientation to the members of the group and the way in which one works with them. Respect occurs when you are "for" the other person, when you regard each person as unique and different from all the rest (the group is first of all a collection of particular individuals, each with unique personalities, needs, thoughts, feelings, etc.). The communication of respect further involves the leader's willingness to work with the individuals within the group, the leader's regard for the individuals' self-determination, and the leader's assumption of the group members' goodwill to the leader and to the others in the group. Communicating your eagerness to work with the members of the group involves paying careful, energetic attention to each person as well as willingness to suspend critical judgment of each one. Respect cultivates the existing and potential resources of all the people in the group and reinforces their active use of their own resources. Accurate empathy, genuineness, and warmth further demonstrate respect for a person.

Using Effective Communication. Communication tools and methods that insure both accuracy and effectiveness need to be employed by the skillful group leader throughout the duration of the group, beginning with Stage I. The use of effective communication skills is important as a model of good communication for the group participants. As with active listening, there are a number of good books and workshops that teach effective communication skills.[10] Particularly important are the skills of "speaking for self" through making "I statements" about specific areas of a person's awareness and experience, reflective listening leading to mutual understanding, and utilizing the style of communication that is most appropriate to the intention of the communicator and the purpose of the group or goal of the relationship. Furthermore, effective communication is enhanced when the communication is given and received in a manner showing respect for and building the dignity and self-regard of each person.

The Social Impact of Effective Leadership

Effective leadership at Stage I does have a potent social influence on the group member. The effective leader is perceived as having social or interpersonal expertise, not only by role definition but by leadership skills—that is, good interpersonal helping behaviors demonstrated within the group. The group leader, and thus the group, is deemed trustworthy, so the participant feels encouraged and is willing to explore himself or herself personally, his or her interpersonal relationships within the group, the content material of the group, and ways to accomplish the tasks or purposes of the group. The participant in a group characterized by effective leadership feels included in the life of the group and develops hope that the group experience will be meaningful and useful. Thus, the participant's motivation for participating is increased. The leader and the group are therefore perceived as attractive. In addition, continued effective group behavior is encouraged, and the group is able to move smoothly through the comple-

---

[10] "Couple Communication" and "Working Together," two workshops developed by Interpersonal Communications Programs, Inc. of Minneapolis, are outstanding in teaching good communication skills. The texts for Couple Communication are *Talking Together I*, Minneapolis: Interpersonal Communication Programs, 1979, and *Alive and Aware*, Minneapolis: Interpersonal Communication Programs, 1975.

tion of this first stage and on to the second stage, the stage of work and growth—toward accomplishing the overall goals and purposes of the group. So far, the group, if it is functioning effectively, has been essentially a pleasurable social experience, and its members are, in varying degrees, eager to continue.

ACTIVE LEARNING EXERCISES FOR
CHAPTER TWO

(1) In triads, have each person present a two-minute self-description to another person in the group; three or four items in a wallet may be useful in forming or documenting that description. Another person practices "attending," including nonattending and overattending, and accurate empathy. One person is a message sender, another is the message receiver and responder, and the third person is an observer. Rotation should provide each person with the opportunity to practice each role. A leader is then selected for the group, and each person is introduced to the small group by his or her partners in the triad. Throughout the practice group, it is important for the leader to consciously employ the skills presented in this chapter. It will be helpful for the participants to observe both the leader's use of these skills (e.g., Does the leader accurately paraphrase a group member's message? Be careful to accurately document your observation!) and the dynamics that appear to be operating. Continue to discuss items of personal interest and concern.

(2) Write a group contract for this learning experience, including a clear statement of purpose, an action plan, how the group is to evaluate its experience, and a concluding celebration.

(3) Contract to do something together as a group outside of the practice or class session. Reflect on what impact this activity has on the group at the next practice group meeting.

(4) Evaluate the leader on each of the leadership skills of Stage I on a scale from 0 to 5 (5 = highly effective; 0 = not effective at all). Using the same rating scale, evaluate how effective the group was in helping you to feel included and eager to work.

chapter three

Stage II—Work: Understanding and Growth

To understand and to grow requires effort. The coach of a swim teach challenged his swimmers with the slogan "No pain, no gain!" Yet, it is the understanding and growth that comes from hard work for which many groups are formed. For those groups formed for a task or a project, understanding and growth are important and necessary ingredients leading to the accomplishment of that task. Usually Stage II is the longest and most dynamic stage of the group's life. Occasionally it is the final or only stage.

Stage II has been described as the transition stage, the movement from the initial phase of coming together toward the action the group or the individual need and/or want to take. It is at this stage that movement takes place for the group or for the individuals involved. The movement or change is not always evident until Stage III, often causing participants to feel bogged down, stuck, frustrated, or confused; yet it can be, and often is, a period of important change and growth. How the dynamics of this stage operate and how skillfully the leader functions will have considerable effect on the productivity and outcome of this phase.

As a group has successfully passed through Stage I and moves into Stage II, the participants, including the leader, sense that the group is settling in and beginning to work through the realities of its ongoing life. The "honeymoon" of Stage I is over, the initial exploring and including phase is past, and the group moves on to the major purpose or task of the group. The cost of continued participation begins to surface, and the needs for growth emerge. This is usually accompanied by some resistance and defensiveness. While influences which work against involvement in the group emerge in Stage II, the opportunities for far greater intimacy, for building close bonds, and for deeper, more dynamic understanding also emerge. The group at this stage is sometimes described as weird, for tensions and intense conflict may develop within the group. Simultaneously, greater warmth and closeness may also emerge. It is an interesting, exciting, productive, and important phase in the group's life.

GROUP DYNAMICS—STAGE II

Group Goal

A change or growth in thinking, feeling, or behavior is the goal of this stage. The process of Stage II is work, work directed toward experiencing dynamic self-understanding and/or growth for each of the participants and/or a dynamic understanding of the subject or task for which the group is formed. What, then, are the dynamics that effect change and growth during this central phase?

Dynamics that Facilitate Understanding and Growth

Cohesiveness—The Key! The central and key dynamic of a group that is working hard toward understanding, change, and growth, or of a group that is directed toward a particular task, is the cohesiveness or "togetherness" of the group. Togetherness is to a group what the relationship is in a one-on-one involvement. Most of the group's eventual success or failure hinges on this dynamic.

Defined and Described. Group cohesiveness is defined by Yalom as that which results from all of the forces acting to get the participants to remain in the group.[1] That is to say, cohesiveness is the attractiveness of the group for each of its members. It is cohesiveness, a sense of togetherness, more than anything else, that gives energy to the group and motivates the individuals toward positive personal and group outcomes. According to Yalom, research in the effectiveness of psychotherapy has demonstrated that those individuals who had positive outcomes in their therapeutic experience had more satisfying relationships than those who did not.

As a therapeutic factor, the experience of being accepted by an individual or by several persons in a group, in spite of one's fantasies of being basically undesirable and unacceptable, has a potent healing and growth-stimulating effect. Membership in a group and the acceptance and approval of others is of utmost importance, both in building healthy lives individually and in building an effectively functioning group that is able to accomplish its purpose. When cohesiveness is missing, feelings of alienation, despair, boredom, and/or irrelevance tend to surface and draw energy away from both the group and the individual participants.

In groups with high levels of togetherness, there is a greater freedom to express conflict and hostility both to the leader and to the other members. It seems as though cohesive groups are less threatened and more able to tolerate intense feelings of conflict between members. This is perhaps due to the fact that there is greater confidence in the strength of the bond in a cohesive group. As conflict surfaces, it needs to be expressed. As it is expressed in a constructive manner, togetherness builds. However, if the conflict is persistent, it can interfere with the group and consume too much of the group's time and energy; thus diverting its energies from the primary function. Wisdom is needed on the part of the group leader in order to decide whether the amount of conflict is within creative parameters.

[1] Yalom, *The Theory and Practice of Group Psychotherapy*, pp. 46–47.

Incidentally, a simple, practical value of group cohesiveness is to be found in the fact that attendance is more frequent and more consistent in groups with high levels of cohesiveness. Furthermore, group members persist in their participation in the group for a longer period of time when there is a high level of togetherness.

In a group that it characterized by high levels of togetherness, group members will:

> work harder to positively influence each other
> be more positively influenced by others
> be more willing to listen to each other
> be more accepting of each other
> feel greater security
> feel less tension
> participate more readily
> honor and protect the group
> be less threatened by the termination of a member or of the group itself.[2]

A cohesive group will have more energy, greater participation, and more responsiveness; therefore, it is likely to achieve desired group and individual goals. In short, a cohesive group will be more effective than a group lacking togetherness.

Since togetherness is that crucial, since cohesiveness is central to the effectiveness of the group, how then does a leader go about building a cohesive group?

Building Togetherness. A sense of togetherness in a group is built, first of all, through making the group rewarding for the participants as individuals. If a leader of the group is aware of what motivates the people in the group and is able to direct the outcome of their participation in the group toward those motivations, cohesiveness will build. It is particularly important that the leader respond to and attempt to meet the motivations of the group members rather than the leader's motivation. If a participant feels pushed by the leader's agenda or by the necessity of satisfying the leader's needs, the group will seem less rewarding to that individual, motivation will

---

[2] Yalom, *The Theory and Practice of Group Psychotherapy*, pp. 66–67.

drop, and cohesiveness will diminish. Incidentally, an aware-ness of Maslow's "hierarchy of needs" will be helpful for the leader in assessing the need level at which each person is functioning, and thus their prime motivation for partici-pating.[3]

As the group members interact with each other, pieces of conversation and experience link together and form chains of common experience, heritage, and culture. Times of laugh-ter and joking, small talk, dramatic moments, humorous inci-dents, and crises all contribute to forming a group history that binds participants together through shared experience. As people share their reminiscences of the group, either within the group sessions or in informal experiences with the group or subgroups outside the group sessions, evidence of a commonness or togetherness is recognized. For example, observe a group of women who were in the same sorority in college recall, almost endlessly, their shared experiences. So too, observe men who were in the armed forces together reminiscing their old war stories. These are signs of a strong bond of shared life that holds these people together. Some groups have informal rites and rituals—for example, humorous contemporary cards for each birthday in the group, alternat-ing responsibility for making certain that there are cookies or doughnuts on hand, periodically going out for coffee or dinner together as a group. All of these shared experiences work together to form a cherished culture and an honored tradition, and to build cohesiveness.

The more the group is identified as a group, as long as individual recognition and value is not eliminated, the greater the sense of togetherness is. Some leaders of functional, task-oriented groups will build a sense of togetherness through having the members wear a uniform, clearly emphasizing not simply their role, but their togetherness as a team, recognized

[3] Maslow listed physiological needs (food and shelter) as most basic. If these were satisfied (or nearly so), a person would then be motivated by needs of security. As security needs are met, an individual is motivated by love, affection, and belonging needs. When belonging needs are met, self-esteem needs, followed by self-actualiza-tion, needs are the motivators. The crowning needs and motivators are the need to understand and know, and aesthetic needs. Abraham Maslow, *Motivation and Personality*, rev. ed. (New York: Harper & Row, 1970).

as such by what they wear. Their common dress visibly binds them together in the same enterprise. These and other ways in which team work can be stressed (such as subgroup or total group cooperation on a project) will help develop a sense of togetherness.

Togetherness is further enhanced by the mutual cooperative setting of clear, attainable, worthwhile goals. This gives the group the hope and conviction that the group is moving in a positive direction, and doing so in a way that is realistic and achievable. If a group's goals are not defined, if they are vague, or if the goals are grandiose and unattainable, despair and lethargy will eventually set in. This is often preceded by an unusual amount of tension, frustration, and conflict. Part of effective goal setting is the recognition and reward of the participants and the leader for achieving those group or individual goals or for enhancing growth and change in positive directions. We know from behavioral psychology that the recognition and reward of desirable behavior encourage repetition. So too, individual and group rewards will build a greater sense of togetherness. Notice, for instance, the difference in togetherness and overall enthusiasm of the defensive unit of a football team that has just had a successful goal line stand, accompanied by the thunderous appreciation of the fans. Their commitment to their shared task develops from such recognition. Usually their performance the next time they are on the field will reflect that commitment.

In the process of building togetherness, it is important to treat each of the members as an individual and not as a mechanical part of an impersonal machine. Individual differences need to be recognized, respected, appreciated, and even encouraged. Furthermore, disagreements and the open expression of conflict need to be tolerated and encouraged. Honest differences need to be dealt with constructively, conveying respect for the value of each individual as well as the group. Even disruptive individuals need to be recognized; yet strong control by the leader or by the group needs to keep the disruptive individual from imposing his or her individuality on the others at the expense of the group or the well being of each member.

Finally, group togetherness is enhanced when people have fun and enjoy their group experience. Many groups are too sober, somber, and sullen. They squelch the spontaneity and simple enjoyment that participation in the group can bring. As a leader or participant in a small group—have fun!

Result. The end result of all this togetherness is the encouragement of and challenge to the participants with regard to the growth. The group which develops a high level of cohesiveness will stimulate interpersonal learning and commitment to the group. Those factors, coupled with an open response to good information, will effect understanding, change, and growth.

Creation of a Family System. The second dynamic that is operating at this stage of a group's life is that of forming relationships within the group that unconsciously reenact the families in which the participants grew up. Yalom calls this "the recapitulation of the primary family."[4] As a group builds bonds of inclusion and togetherness and settles into a long-term life (more than four to eight sessions), participants more and more relate to each other in ways similar to the ways in which they related to people not only in their current families, but to the individuals in their families of origin. Although this is done unconsciously, it profoundly affects the ways in which people relate to and work with others in the group. Someone in the group has a leadership role that is unconsciously reminiscent of the leadership of father or mother or someone else in the primary family. Another group member is experienced to be nurturing in a way similar to Mom or Dad or an older sibling. Someone else in the group triggers feelings one had for a competitive brother or sister. Usually, members relate to a designated leader or the natural leader (if different from the appointed leader) as the "mother" or "father" of the group (unless someone else assumes that role), and to other group members as siblings. The group becomes an occasional family, and the longer and more intensively the group meets, the more like family it becomes. Note, for

---

[4] Yalom, *The Theory and Practice of Group Psychotherapy*, pp. 14–15.

example, how often a professional athletic team refers to itself as family (like the Pittsburgh Pirates in 1979).

The presence of this dynamic is rooted in the understanding that human personality is formed primarily in a small group (the family), and is changed through or shaped through participation in other small group experiences (whether formal or informal). We first learn how to communicate, understand ourselves, play our role or function, and relate to others on the basis of our repeated experiences at home. All subsequent social encounters are either a reenactment or reshaping of those primary relationships. Thus, while participants can get locked into repetitive, predictable responses and behaviors within one group, or from group to group (have you noticed, for instance, how often a person who has a problem in one setting will have the same problem in a new setting?), they can also learn and utilize new responses and new behaviors in the group and transfer that change to other settings as well. The group is a powerful instrument to elicit old, ingrained patterns—and to change them!

Family Systems Theory[5] has made a marvelous contribution to our understanding of how people function in groups. Emphasis in family systems is on the system and the roles people fill in order to help the system operate in an orderly, functional way. The system, the organism, as it develops has needs that the members, as they join the system, must fulfill for the system to live and thrive. Consciously (rarely) or unconsciously (usually), the system assigns roles or functions to each participant. The roles help to ensure the continuation of the system and its balance or homeostasis. This happens in a primary family, and it happens in a secondary family (a small group). The group will thus have group mothers and fathers and siblings, perhaps a grandparent or aunt or uncle, and often a pet or mascot. The more rigid and inflexible the group is, the more rigid, inflexible, and stereotyped the roles within it are. A healthy group is rather mobile and adaptable in these roles, and the greater the flexibility in existence, the greater the opportunity for change and growth is.

In systems theory, the focus is on the individual only in

---

[5] See the bibliography on Family Systems.

the context of the system. The individual person is understood primarily in terms of the role he or she plays. For problems that emerge in the system, the focus is not primarily on the individual manifesting the problem, but on the entire system. If a child is acting out inappropriately, rather than focusing almost exclusively on the child's problem, a systems approach would seek to understand the problem within the context of the system—what function does it have, what stimulates or elicits the problem, what would happen if the problem was not there, and so on. In a small group that is deeply into Stage II, with a participant who is behaving in a way that is disruptive to the group and interfering with its progress, the attention is directed toward the group and what is happening in the group to stimulate that reaction. This approach, incidentally, does not eliminate the individual from taking personal responsibility for her or his behavior, but tries to understand it in a larger context.

Virginia Satir has identified and described four basic roles that people play in a family (or in a group).[6] One role is that of "Hero" or "Blamer." This is the person who assumes a position of power by challenging, confronting, or blaming others. This person is often evidenced by pointing a finger or using words like "You ought . . . ," "If you only . . . ," "If it weren't for . . . ," "Shame on you . . . ," "I've worked so hard, how could you . . . ," thus controlling the conversation and the emotional and relational atmosphere. A blamer needs a "Placator" or "Scapegoat." This is the shame-oriented person who often has a whiney tone and punctuates his or her replies with "I'm so sorry . . . ," "But I was only trying to help . . . ," and tries very hard to please. Yet, at the same time, placators are often defending, rationalizing, and justifying themselves and/or their actions. The "Lost Child" or "Super Reasonable" person fills a third role in the family system. This is the intellectualizer who stays emotionally and personally detached from what is happening when a group is not functioning well. He or she copes with stress by acting "above it all" and/or dealing with specific issues in very abstract or generalized ways. A fourth role in a dysfunctional family, according to Satir, is

---

[6] Virginia Satir, *Peoplemaking* (Palo Alto: Science and Behavior Books, 1972).

that of the "mascot" or "irrelevant person." This is the person whose function seems to be that of a pressure valve, releasing the tension by drawing the focus to themselves in a relatively benign, often cute, humorous, silly, and/or superficial and inappropriate (though sometimes appreciated) way.

In a healthy group, as in a healthy family, these roles are not rigidly determined. There is a considerable amount of shifting in these roles, as well as additional roles that are much more supportive to the health of the system. When a group struggles and becomes increasingly dysfunctional, there is a strong likelihood that these roles have become rigid, and the individuals and the group are "stuck."

Yet, a stuck group can become unstuck as the roles switch or are replaced with new roles. As one or more people in the group change their roles or learn and use new ones, the others are pushed by the system to change their roles. Thus, the group's "family" atmosphere has enormous power to effect change as well as to perpetuate the old patterns.

It is important that the leader of a small group discourage the dysfunctional or maladaptive behavior of a participant who, either directly or indirectly, tries to take control of the group. If the leader does not discourage this, the entire group will have a strong tendency to arrange itself as a system to support and encourage this participant's dominance, leading to the frustration, discouragement, and detriment of the group and its primary task. A considerable amount of time can be diverted from the group's purpose by a person acting out an inappropriate behavior. This new "family," the group, can provide this person with responses that differ from those experienced in the family of origin or in other groups where the behavior was expressed. Furthermore, the members of the group, including the leader, can be models of alternative behaviors of people who do not play this person's games.

Through the unwillingness of other members of the group to play complementary roles, this person's behavior and role are challenged. Thus the group can create friction, frustration, or hostility in this person, especially if he or she lacks the insight or motivation to change or finds change painful and undesirable. As an extreme reaction, this person may quit the group, placing considerable blame on the others (directly or indirectly) for not meeting his or her needs or expectations. However, if the leader and the group can supportively work with this person, avoid getting trapped into playing the complementary role, act objectively, and ride through the "storms," this participant's behavior is likely to change. Incidentally, it is helpful for group leaders to be aware of the role(s) they tend to play in groups and reflect on its similarity to the role(s) they learned in their original families. For a leader who is working with a troublesome member, reality testing, objectifying the conversation, asking for data regarding feelings, thoughts, wants, and subject matter should continually be encouraged.

Learning From Each Other.   A third group dynamic that is operative in Stage II is what Yalom refers to as "Interpersonal learning."[7] Through a person's involvement in a small group, that person is involved in several important, interpersonal relationships. Through those relationships, learning occurs.

Interpersonal relationships are important. They are, as Harlow's experiments with monkeys demonstrated, necessary for survival. As we have noted, Abraham Maslow lists "belonging" as a basic need (right after psychological and safety needs). A songwriter has said that those who know they need other people are the luckiest people of all. William James said, "We are not only gregarious animals liking to be in sight of our fellows, but we have innate propensity to get ourselves noticed, and noticed favorably, by our kind. No more fiendish punishment could be devised, were such a thing possible, then that one should be turned loose in society and remain absolutely unnoticed by all the members thereof."[8]

Our self-concept is based in part on the perceived appraisals of others. We define who we are largely in reaction to the response others give to us, beginning with mother and family members, then peers in school and neighborhood, and

---

[7] Yalom, *The Theory and Practice of Group Psychotherapy,* p. 19.

[8] William James, *The Principles of Psychology,* Vol. I (New York: Henry Hall, 1890), p. 293.

others in our ever-widening contacts as we grow. Throughout life, peer appraisal is a potent force for good or evil, depending on its motive and use. An important goal for personal maturity is to understand oneself so well that the person known to self is the same person that is known to others. Putting it in the concept of the Johari Window, an important personal objective is to maximize that section of myself that is open and known both to me and to others, and to minimize my blind spots (known to others, but not to me), and hidden or facade (known to me, but not to others).[9] Or, as Jourard would put it, to be a "Transparent Self."[10]

Relationships with others in a group can be a powerfully corrective emotional experience as a participant changes and tries on a new behavior, new attitudes, new feelings, and so on. In the context of a small group, people who are growing and changing can check out the appropriateness of their new understanding through testing it in the "real world" of the small group and observing the response of others. There are several critical moments in a group where change can be encouraged or stifled. When a participant shows strong negative feelings, or even strong positive feelings (feelings of unusual warmth and joy), the group's response to that individual is critical to that incident being used as a growing experience for that person. This is particularly true if the expression of those strong feelings is new to that person or to the group. How a group responds to a woman who has never before admitted to or expressed anger will profoundly affect whether she will be open to the appropriate expresssion of that emotion in the future. How the group responds to a man who weeps for the first time as he becomes aware of and allows himself to experience grief over a loss will profoundly affect his willingness to openly display that emotion in the future. If a person in a group, whether in a therapy group or in a task-oriented group, takes a positive risk in making a new self-disclosure and is ignored or criticized, that individual is less likely to take that risk again. On the other hand, if someone takes a risk, tries something new, and gets positive feedback, that

---

[9] Joseph Luft, *Group Process: An Introduction to Group Dynamics* (Palo Alto: Mayfield Publishing Company, 1970)
[10] Sidney Jourard, *The Transparent Self* (Princeton: D. Van Nostrand, 1964).

member is much more likely to take that risk again; thus, change and growth will occur.

The small group is a microcosmic society for each participant. As the group continues to meet, not only will the participants reenact their families of origin, but each member will increasingly create the same kind of interpersonal relationships that he or she currently has outside the group. Thus, if a person has difficulty in a certain relationship or demonstrates inappropriate behavior outside the group, eventually those difficulties and behaviors will manifest themselves in the group. Therefore, a major challenge to a group that meets for a considerable time will be to effectively deal with the inappropriate behavior and relationship conflicts that develop in a way that is helpful both to the individual and to the process and purpose of the group. Little can be done within the group to resolve a member's problem outside the group, but by focusing on the "here and now" dynamics within the group, the same kinds of problems can be dealt with to the individual's benefit. Thus, it is very important to keep the focus of attention on what is happening within the group. Also, the "here and now" focus has a powerful influence on what that person does outside the group. Behavior learned within the group can and often does tranfer outside the group to other relationships and settings.

Thus, the learning-from-each-other dynamic of a small group in the second stage of its life can also provide important insight for the participants. First, a small group member has the potential of gaining a more objective perspective on their interpersonal behavior. In a group we learn more about how others see and understand us. Secondly, a group member can gain increased understanding of the effect of his or her actions on others by observing their responses. Then too, a person's intentions and motivations are often discovered through these relationships and the effect one's behavior has on the others in the group.

Imitating the Leader. A fourth dynamic of a Stage II group is that of imitating the skilled leader. People in a group will tend to imitate the behavior, the attitudes, and even mannerisms of both the leader (particularly the natural leader) and other members of the group. This can, of course, have either good or negative impact on the group, depending upon the effectiveness of that leader's behavior on the group process. If the imitated leader or mimiked group member is making positive contributions to the group and is living an effectively functioning, healthy life outside the group, this can be a very positive, helpful dynamic of a group. On the other hand, a leader's or group member's dysfunction can also be transmitted to a group. Yet, a group provides the participants will more than one model; thus the imitative behavior can be diffused over the entire group.

Transition, Evaluation, Adjustments. As a group progresses into and through this second phase of its life, numerous transition or midlife stress points occur. The group and the participants are moving from a concept or vision through the realities of an existing group that is evolving or developing into something that inevitably is in some contrast to the original vision or concept. Theory and dream must make way for the concrete realities. In the process, an occasional evaluation of the group goals, norms, process, contract, and effectiveness needs to be made. Does the group seem to be moving toward its basic objectives and goals? Are those goals still desirable and achievable? Is the group process and are the rules enabling the group to move systematically or persistently in the direction of achieving those goals? Is the group enjoyable or desirable for the participants? These and other questions need to be raised to assess the group's progress. In so doing, certain adjustments in the group's life may need to be made to increase the likelihood of the group's purpose being reached.

As indicated, this should be done occasionally. If evaluation is made too frequently, group members often become disenchanted with the group, believing too much effort is spent on group self-assessment. Furthermore, the group can become self-absorbed and drain its energies away from its primary purpose. Infrequent or nonexistent evaluation can lead a group into obliviousness regarding its life; thus the group and/or the group leader fails to make those adjustments which would enhance the group's effectiveness. A healthy balance of monthly or quarterly group evaluation is helpful.

Leadership Goals

Leadership for a second stage group is more complex than for a first stage group. In addition to the skills needed at Stage II, the leader continues to need the skills that were useful and important at Stage I, for the second stage builds on and includes the dynamics of the first stage. Throughout this second stage the group leader needs to carry out the leadership functions and skills of Stage I, but now adds to them the new functions and skills of this stage. While there are new goals for this stage, the leader continues to need to facilitate kindness, stimulate discovery, positively effect good communication, and communicate genuineness, respectfulness, empathy, and attentiveness. The leader continues to give direct leadership in Stage II, but in a manner somewhat different from that of Stage I. Now the skilled group leader begins to transfer some of the responsibility for directing the group to the other group members and increasingly works to share the leadership with them. This changing leadership function, as the leader turns more of the control over to the group itself, can be diagramed as follows (assuming a group with an appointed leader):

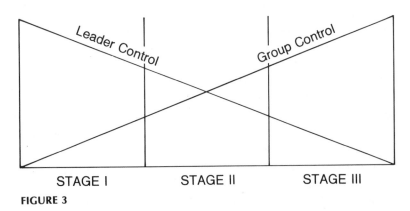

FIGURE 3

The primary function of the leader at this second level is to continue to facilitate the group's movement toward the goals of integration, the evocation of understanding, and en-

couraging and stimulating change, growth, and progress. The
leader at Stage II works hard both at integrating the group
members (helping to build togetherness) and at integrating
the material or content of the group. A leader at this second
level also strives to effect a dynamic understanding of the
individuals within the group, the content around which the
group is functioning, and the group process. The skilled leader
tries to keep his or her focus on the "big picture"—a "global"
perspective of the group itself—while working to maintain
intensive attention to each individual. In short, the leader's
goal or function at Stage II is to provide encouragement to
each individual as well as to the group as a whole.

With encouragement, the group members will invest
themselves in the group task and process. Both the leader
and the group are involved in hard work at this stage, and
both need encouragement to continue the effort. Most change
is hard work and often appears risky and scary. Inertia tends
to keep people and groups from making major changes. Yet,
with relaxed persistence and gentle persuasion (i.e., encouragement), they often do evidence change and growth.

Leadership skills

Advanced Empathy—Implicit and/or Context.   The most basic skill that is needed for Stage II of a group's life is what
Gerard Egan has labeled "Advanced Accurate Empathy."[11]
In the previous chapter, we discussed primary empathy,
where the empathic understanding and response is in response to the overt and explicit message of that person. Advanced empathy focuses on the covert and implicit message
of that person. The former deals with the content of a person's
statement, while the latter looks more at the inner-personal
and interpersonal context. Advanced empathy considers the
implications of another's words, themes, tone, behavior, facial
expressions, and function or role in a system and evaluates
what meaning these might have to that person. The goal in
this more advanced empathy, this investigation of the implicit

[11] Egan, *The Skilled Helper,* p. 36.

message, is to help the person move beyond self-or subject exploration to self-or subject understanding. This self-understanding is, of course, a dynamic self-understanding. People are not static and unchanging, rather, they are usually in some form of movement. Hopefully, our self-perceptions are changing as we grow to more accurate and complete self-awareness. Advanced empathy gets to the feelings and meanings that are below the surface, that is, the hidden meaning and message behind the person's stated message.

With advanced accurate empathy, as with primary accurate empathy, emphasis needs to be placed on the word "accurate." It is crucially important that the message the leader hears from a group member is the same message that the member sends. It is extremely easy for a leader to read more into a person's message or behavior than was meant or said, thus leaving the other person feeling misunderstood, or worse, not listened to and not appreciated. The message heard and responded to needs to be the same as the message that was sent. It needs to be accurate. Thus, advanced accurate empathy should be expressed tentatively yet courageously, respectfully recognizing that no one, including the effective leader of a small group, is able to get a perfectly precise reading of another person's mind.

Verbalizing What Is Implied. With recognition of that caution, "advanced accurate empathy" can be expressed through stating to the other that which is only implied in his or her statement. In so doing, it is very helpful, if not necessary, for the empathic person to document his or her tentative response, pointing to tone of voice, facial expression, body language, behavioral responses, repetitive actions, and listing what you have observed that has led you to that conclusion as to the hidden meanings. Remember, the skilled leader is not a mind reader; instead, the leader is a reader of behavioral signs that form a message. We will usually know the accuracy of our empathic response through some kind of nonverbal clue, such as a smile, a nod, a sigh, or a "Yeah," "Uh Huh," "Sure," "You bet," "Really," that signifies the acceptance of our response.

Making Connections. Building a bridge to link scattered

segments of information, thought, or conversation into a connected, unified whole is another means of conveying "advanced accurate empathy."[12] What on the surface appears to be a series of disconnected statements and thoughts often forms a mosaic or mural with a recurring theme, and the skillful leader can connect these seemingly isolated experiences or thoughts.

Pointing Out Logical Conclusions. Furthermore, the effective small group leader can facilitate self-understanding through communicating accurate empathy by helping a group member draw conclusions from premises. From a series of statements by the group member, the effective listener can draw out the logical sequence and implications of the group member's statements or actions. Occasionally this can be done "tongue in cheek" by carefully leading the group member to conclusions the leader knew were contrary to that person's expectation. However, if one followed the logic of the member's own statements, the outcome would be quite different from what the member presumed or expected. A further tool for conveying advanced empathy is the movement from the less to the more, from the individual incident and statement, the fragmentary element, to testing out broader, more general meanings and perspectives.

Summarizing Central Theme. Another way for the group leader to communicate "advanced accurate empathy," according to Egan, is through stating a summary of the basic core material that has been presented.[13] This is done through observing and identifying a continuing or central theme running through the member's statements and behaviors. Pointing out these common themes adds a sense of movement and clarity to a conversation and helps the leader, the person making the statement, and the group itself feel that there is a direction in which the group is moving. Summary, while used most often at the conclusion of a group session, can also be used to begin a new session or as a review in the middle of a group, in order to help an individual or the group itself come to some new awareness and understanding. In addition,

[12] Egan, *The Skilled Helper*, p. 144.
[13] Egan, *The Skilled Helper*, p. 137.

summary can be used to stimulate and make smooth a transition point in the session. Occasionally it is useful for the group members, collectively as well as individually, to summarize their own material, leaning toward their own self-understanding.

Tentative and Documented. Skilled and seasoned as some group leaders and empathic people are, it is always important for the leader to start with primary empathy, and only after responding in primary empathy should that leader move toward the use of advanced empathy. Throughout the communication of empathy, caution and tentativeness need to be attached to the empathic response. However, clear, concise documentation of that other person's behavior adds considerable weight to the leader's insight.

Confrontation. One of the most frequently used and abused skills at this level of group life is that of confrontation. Much has been said, pro and con, about the usefulness of confrontation. There has not been the positive correlation between confrontation and positive change or growth in individuals that the proponents of confrontation would suggest (except in some behavior modification programs). Nevertheless, it represents a useful Stage II leadership skill. Important to an effective use of confrontation is a base of trust and genuine care and concern for the person being confronted—that is, respect or even love. Caution and tentativeness are crucial to that base of respect and trust in which an effective confrontation can take place. A willingness on the part of the confronter to become more deeply involved with the one confronted is necessary in order for the confrontation to have its maximum impact.

Use of Confrontation. The effective employment of confrontation in a small group depends on the relationship of the confrontation to the overall group purpose. If it helps effect understanding, change, and personal growth, without diverting energies from other crucial tasks, confrontation will be useful; otherwise, it can be counterproductive. A confrontation should be directed to the goal of helping a group member develop greater understanding of self and the impact of his or her behavior on others. Furthermore, confrontation can be with positive as well as negative material. Not only can self-destructive personal, interpersonal, or group interfering behavior be confronted, but also strengths, achievements, personal growth, and behaviors which are helpful to the group can be confronted. In fact, a confrontive affirmation usually has greater impact on the growth and development of individuals than does a critical confrontation. Not only should discrepancies, distractions, games, evasions, inconsistencies, and incongruities be confronted, but also, assets, abilities, new insights, positive behaviors, evident growth, observed skills, or simply the potential for growth and accomplishment should be confronted or affirmed.

The Manner of Confrontation. Whatever is confronted, whether that which is negative or that which is positive and hopeful, that which needs to be corrected, or that which needs to be encouraged, all confrontation should be in proportion to the relationship between the confronter and the person being confronted. That is to say, the confronter needs to assess the amount of trust and willingness of the leader to be personally involved, and the confronting leader should take into consideration the capacity of the "confrontee" to receive the confrontation.

Furthermore, the confronting leader needs to observe the response of the person being confronted. Does that person deny the confrontation? Does he or she argue and challenge the confrontation or seek to discredit it? Does the individual seek the support of others in the group in opposition to the confrontation? Does the confronted participant carefully absorb and examine the validity of the statement? That is, does the "confrontee" give careful consideration to the confrontation in a way that will be helpful and stimulate growth? In some ways, the entire group process toward growth and understanding is a continuing confrontation and challenge; this confrontation is necessarily involved.

Leader Disclosure. A third leadership skill at this stage is that of self-disclosure: the capacity to reveal yourself to or share something about yourself with the other members of the group. While research appears contradictory as to its effec-

has great value in objectifying and building confidence in that interpretation. Incidentally, this is a useful way of helping persons develop greater tolerance toward others, particularly those with whom they disagree. This helps a person learn to disagree without defensiveness, antagonism, or an unnecessary rigidity that would interfere with building healthy relationships.

Most people facing a particular situation in their lives have options, whether they are aware of them or not. Enabling persons to see the alternatives helps them to recognize and make choices rather than feel helplessly that their options are taken away and they are unable to choose. Incidentally, this also increases healthy personal responsibility, for I must take responsibility for the choices I make. I cannot cop out by saying "I couldn't help it!" or "The devil made me do it!" To live is to choose—and the choices are there.

This completes Stage II—perhaps the most important, and certainly the largest and most demanding phase of a group's life. Stage II is hard work, for it involves the work of developing a dynamic, living understanding by each person. The goal of this second level is change and growth. Stage II can take a long time to complete, perhaps two or more years for a group that meets regularly. It is like climbing a mountain with false peaks, discouraging, demoralizing valleys, hard uphill climbs, rocks to stumble over, and crises to handle. Often, (even usually if the group is progressing effectively) new, interesting, exciting vistas, new understanding, and new growth await the group member in this stage. It is well worth the effort, and even the effort itself can become enjoyable. Remember—as Stage II progresses, more and more of the responsibility for the group is shared by the group itself. This can be a wonderful partnership, a collaborative effort, teammates working together toward a common goal.

ACTIVE LEARNING EXERCISES FOR CHAPTER THREE

(1) Create a family map by drawing circles representing each person in your family of origin, varying the size of the circle

in terms of the person's importance within the family, and arranging them according to your perceptions of the closeness of the various relationships within the family. Give each person a symbolic color to represent his or her emotional impact on the family.

(2) Assign one of Satir's four family roles to each of the persons in your family of origin, including yourself (recognizing that these roles are rarely rigid and constant). Now, assign one of Satir's four family roles to each of the persons in your practice group. Who in your practice group do you have the greatest difficulty relating to? Is there any similarity between this person and someone in your family of origin? Does this provide you with any insights into the way you relate to these persons in this practice group? Together as a group, assign each person in the group to a primary role based on your shared perceptions and dramatize these roles. Discuss with the practice leader the feeling each of you had as you dramatized these roles. What insight or growth stimulus did it provide for you?

(3) In triads, practice your confrontation skills by confronting one of the persons in the triad with the *effects* of one aspect of that person's behavior that interferes with the group process, utilizing all of the leadership skills that have been presented thus far.

Repeat the confrontation with the effects of one aspect of that person's behavior that makes a positive contribution to the group process.

(4) Rotating the role of practice leader, discuss each person's response to the statements, "The aspect of small group leadership or participation that I have the greatest difficulty with is _____," "A leadership skill that I feel very confident in and enjoy using is _____," or any other subject matter that is current and personal for the people in the group.

It may be useful in this exercise to have one person function as the practice leader and two others as observers, with the rest as participants.

(5) Rate each practice leader on a 0 to 5 scale on each of the leadership skills discussed in Stages I and II.

Rate the group on a 0 to 5 scale as to its cohesiveness. Reflect on each of the ingredients in cohesiveness and the extent to which each is included or missing in this practice small group.

chapter four

Trouble Shooting— Dealing Creatively with Group Problems

Even the best groups encounter difficulties. Perhaps there has never been a group that has survived for more than a few weeks (especially a group that has moved through Stage II) that has not had to face problems with a group member, group leadership, group process, or a combination of all three. Before we discuss Stage III, we need to look at some of the problems that emerge in the life of a group and suggest ways that the leader and/or the group can cope effectively with and hopefully resolve these problems. While they can emerge at any particular point in the group's life, problems in the group are most likely to occur during Stage II.

Sources of Group Problems

Difficulties in groups can arise over conflicts in the expectations which the participants and the leader have for the group, or among the participants themselves. Almost everyone comes to the group with some expectation of what that group experience will be like for them and what they want and anticipate receiving from their participation. Some of these expectations are conscious and occasionally they are stated. Many are held quietly; some expectations are held unconsciously. Unless the purpose of the group is very limited and the expectations clearly and thoroughly discussed, it is unlikely that there will be a total uniformity of expectations. Furthermore, some of the unstated expectations are likely to be grandiose and quite unrealistic, yet very real for the person or persons holding them. In addition, the group leader and the group members often have differing expectations for the group.

There can also be difficulties emerging from differences in the understanding of the explicit or implicit group contract—what kind of commitment, responsibilities, group structure, and group norms will guide the life of the group and its members over the duration of the group. Often a hidden agenda belonging either to the leader or to one or more of the group members emerges after the group has negotiated its primary objectives and launched its existence. Moreover, leadership competition frequently develops within a group, either between the stated leader and a natural leader within the group, between more than one natural leader, or between co-leaders; thus a power struggle emerges. Related to problems of leadership are problems concerning the use of or response to authority. Often there are personality conflicts between between members of the group or between the leader and a participant. Frequently there are problems arising from the personal needs or interpersonal style of a group member which interferes with the effective functioning of the total group. Sometimes there are stumbling blocks in the dynamics of the group or a dysfunctioning in the "family system" of the small group.

Problems or Opportunities

These problems can be highly destructive to the effectiveness of the group. Certainly they represent an important challenge. Yet, these same problems can also be significant, even exciting opportunities for understanding, renewal, and growth. They can help "make" as well as "break" a group. The hope is that through the discussion that follows, you as a group leader or participant can help turn the problems that emerge in the group from seeds of destruction to seeds of growth.

PROBLEM GROUP MEMBERS

A problem group member is often very obvious. The participant's behavior interferes with the effective functioning of the group and it is easily observed. However, sometimes a group member is creating a problem for the group, and it is not clear who is creating the problem or what that problem is; yet, there is a sense that something is not going right, that something or someone is interfering with effective group process. At times group apathy will reflect the fact that an individual group member is creating a problem for the whole group that has not yet been dealt with in a creative way. Nine such problems group members are discussed below.

The Constant Talker

In many groups there are one or two people who continually charge, like a bull in a china shop, into verbally monopolizing the group's attention. They often start the conversation in the group before the leader begins and frequently volunteers lengthy, energetic, and verbose comments on nearly all subjects. Usually they are quite adapt at gracefully getting into and taking control of a conversation, thereby making it difficult for attention to be focused on anyone or anything else in the group. The dominating person is very common to small groups. Early in the life of a group (in the first session or two at the most!), he or she might be quite useful in helping a group to open up and begin talking. The dominating person takes the pressure off more reserved, timid, or quiet members, allowing them time to build the rapport and trust needed for venturing into the conversation. Dominators can get things going. Yet, sooner or later, they become very disruptive to the group's development, as well as frustrating to deal with for the leader and the other group members.

Early in the group's life (Stage I) it is very important for the leader to control the dominating person and use that individual's participation constructively. An effective small group leader needs to walk a steady line between a weak, passive leadership that allows the dominator to monopolize the group to his or her presumed benefit at the group's expense, and an abrupt seizure of control from the dominator which can be experienced as a put-down of both the dominating person and the group as a whole. A tactful, yet firm control needs to be exercised by the group leader. Later in the group's life (second half of Stage II), the leader can shift responsibility for handling the monopolist to the group and ask the group to take responsibility for dealing with the life of the group and this person's effect on it.

Early in its life the group is often afraid to deal openly and directly with the monopolizer; therefore, that person is allowed to get away with his or her behavior (incidently, that is how others have responded to the monopolizer in the past—thus the development of the monopolizing behavior). Yet, as the constant talking continues, group members become increasingly frustrated and angry. When a group's frustration level increases, one of the following three responses are likely for the individual participant: an outburst of anger toward the monopolizer, directing anger toward some other subject or person (i.e., scapegoating), or a withdrawal into apathy and diminished participation. None of these alternatives are helpful to the group process. In fact, they are obstacles at best and potentially destructive. Thus, until the group is ready to manage itself and its own members, the leader needs to exercise firm, sensitive, skilled leadership. But how?

A skilled leader, first of all, avoids getting drawn into a power struggle where she or he is competing with the dominator for control of the group. To do so acknowledges, supports, and in a way gives in to the monopolizer's quest for dominance. While the leader may occasionally need to firmly and forcibly silence the dominator and take control, usually this can be done in a manner that facilitates effective group process. There are two basic ways to do so. First, the leader can observe and vocalize to the group the process or the dynamics of what is happening in the group. The leader can use the skill of "immediacy" or the skills of imparting information and concreteness in talking nonjudgmentally about what is happening within the group Second, the skilled leader can help the monopolizing person to observe his or her own behavior, focusing not on the rightness or wrongness of that behavior and that person, but on the effects of that behavior on the leader and on the group as a whole. This is a confrontation, and what is being confronted is the person's behavior, not his personhood. The monopolizing person is not being confronted with the wrongness of his or her behavior, statements, or attitude, but with the effect these have on others. This needs to be done in an open, clear, uncritical, and nonblaming manner. The confrontation is like holding a mirror for the person and letting him or her see the reflection of his or her own actions.

If the problem behavior is effecting the group's life, it is usually best to confront the person within the context of the group. For some, it will only be upon hearing the feedback from several people that belief in and acceptance of the reality and validity of the confrontation will occur. Yet, there may be occasions when it would be more effective to make the confrontation privately, outside the group. Both the needs of the individual and the needs of the group ned to be held in tension with the purpose of the group taking priority.

Sometimes the dominator is simply a supercharged, energetic, enthusiastic person who is unusually highly motivated. In those instances, the leader needs to support and encourage that person's enthusiasm, yet control her or his energy flow in the group so as to utilize that energy for the group and not allow it to become counterproductive. Often this can be done by instructing the enthusiastic member on how to utilize that energy more effectively, and enlisting this person's support of the leader—that is, enlisting the participant as an ally rather than thinking of him or her as an enemy.

The Moralizer

The moralizer has a need to be right and a need to have another person be wrong. The moralizing can be about a variety of subjects and is not limited to what are typically considered moral or religious issues—for example, the right way to fix coffee, or what is wrong with a football team that has

lost three games in a row. The moralizer is usually quite argumentative. However, the self-righteous person, or moralist,
will sometimes express his or her "rightness" in subtle, nonverbal ways that leave the distinct impression that "you're wrong
and I'm right." While these people usually act in a manner
suggestive of their superiority, their self-righteousness is often
a mask for low self-esteem. Frequently they are bothered by
feelings of shame and/or suppressed hostility and are, conse-
quently, tender and easily hurt. In fact, their rigid moralizing
(or self-righteousness) may be an unconscious defense against
ambiguity, uncertainty, or perceived threats to their well-being.

Thus the moralizer needs to be dealt with in a sensitive,
caring, yet firm way. While it is easy for another person, particularly the leader of the group, to get caught up in a debate
about the particular topic on which the moralist is moralizing
(this argumentative, critical, judgmental style of communication has a tremendous power to pull objective and reflective
styles of communication into this controlling style), such a
debate should be avoided and firmly and persistently resisted.
Rather, the leader, by using a more objective style, by raising
questions of information and data gathering, and by using
the skill of self-disclosure, can do much to defuse the disruptive
influence of the moralist on the group's life. As with the dominator, the small group leader can confront the moralist, gently
and tentatively yet firmly, with the effect of his or her behavior
on the group and on individuals within the group. Furthermore, the use of "Alternative Frames of Reference" discussed
in the preceding chapter can be very helpful to encourage
the self-righteous moralizer to be more objective. Most of all,
however, the effective small group leader needs to stay calm
and avoid getting caught in the right/wrong, win/lose game
of the moralist.

The Leader's Assistant

Frequently in small groups there is a person who assumes
the role of leader's assistant, without solicitation and with the
irritation of the others. This person may be skilled and have
much to offer the group, if only it were contributed in a more

acceptable or helpful way. Often, however, the leader's assistant feels some insecurity and limited self-worth and assumes the role as a way of gaining the acceptance and approval of the leader and/or the other members of the group. This is an attempt on the part of this person to prove value, to himself or herself or to others, in a secondhand way, through identification with the group leader.

Such a person can generate considerable interaction within the group and can occasionally make an important contribution; yet the leader's assistant often verbally hides behind the leader while the group becomes increasingly frustrated and irritated. When this happens it is often difficult to reach this member and lead him or her into the mainstream of the group. Obviously, the longer the leader's assistant is allowed to maintain this role in the group, the more entrenched the person becomes in that role, and the more difficult it is to lead this participant into a more appropriate role. Thus it is important to intervene early with the leader's assistant, using the skills of confrontation (with the effects of her or his behavior), "immediacy," or self-disclosure, in an atmosphere of personal encouragement.

The Persistent Complainer

A typical member of many small groups is the person who readily and frequently requests the help of the group or the leader but then rejects it. This rejection may be very open and blatant, or quite subtle and difficult to discern. The persistent complainer is the person who frequently responds to suggestions and encouragement by saying "Yes, but . . . ," following with a series of excuses as to why he or she cannot incorporate the suggestion. The persistent complainer can be the person who agrees to do something and is grateful to others for their interest and concern, yet rarely, if ever, reports that he or she has integrated the help offered and made movements toward change and growth. At first, the group and the leader enthusiastically respond to a person who so openly and readily requests help. Yet his or her repeated failure or resistance to follow through with the help eventually leads to frustration, discouragement, boredom, and/or irritation on the part of those who gave the help. Then, as the persistent complainer, after rejecting help, continues (and often increases) complaining, frequently blaming others for his or her failure or even lack of effort, the group's frustration builds.

Usually this person is a passive, dependent person who subtly manipulates others, especially people who are eager care givers, into giving what these caring people are so eager to give—sympathy, advice, suggestions, and help. The persistent complainer is like a person who is thirsty going to a well and asking for water—then walking a few feet away and throwing it on the ground, only to return, complaining of thirst and asking for more water. After this participant has gone to the well over and over and over, the well feels dry and frustrated that the person has come back yet again for more of the same with no apparent utilization of the good help previously offered.

Psychologically these problem people in a small group often have highly conflicting feelings regarding their dependency needs. On the one hand they feel and act dependent and come looking, again and again, for help; on the other hand, they maintain their tenuous autonomy by rejecting help. Such people need not only confrontation and "immediacy," but also strong support with the feedback of "advanced accurate empathy" to come to a greater understanding of their behavior and its affect on others and on themselves.

The Psychotic

A person who is in an active psychotic condition is not likely to gain very much from participation in any group and is usually disruptive to a group's effectiveness. Some people who are controlling their schizophrenia through medication and are not in an active psychotic state can function in some groups and make good contributions to the group. Others do not function well in small groups and not only disrupt the effectiveness of the group but find little benefit from their participation except for the socializing that occurs. The group leader will need to evaluate each situation on the basis of the purpose of the group and the capacity of that person to function effectively within the group.

The Quiet Person

A person who is extremely quiet within a group presents another interesting problem for the group leader. Usually, but not always, the silent member is much less disruptive than the constant talker or assistant leader. However, he or she is certainly challenging. To work effectively with the silent member, it is important to have some sense of the role or function of that person's silence. Is this person basically shy, quiet, reserved? Does he or she feel inadequate, or simply have nothing to contribute—no needs, no resources? Is there a subtle manipulation in disguise that is effected by the silence? Think for example of the influence, the actual power, that totally quiet, sulking, pouting people have in triggering the anxious concern of those close to them. Silence can be golden, and it also can be loaded with manipulative power. Thus it is important to understand the effect of the silence on others and the function of the participant's silence for that person and for the group. Is it a comfortable silence, helping the overall flow of the group; or is it an uncomfortable silence, attracting the attention of the group and stimulating a feeling of anxiety within the group? Confrontation, "advanced accurate empathy," and "immediacy" are all skills that can be used to deal with the manipulative silence.

Some silence, on the other hand, is simple shyness, fear, anxiety, and therefore nonmanipulative. Because such a person is quiet does not mean that he or she is not participating and not receiving something significant through careful listening and applying the group experience to his or her own life. Such a person should be encouraged (again gently) to speak and verbally participate. This person can be drawn out by asking for his or her opinion on the immediate subject of conversation, by assigning the person something to bring to the group at its next session (provided he or she is not isolated by being the only one in that assignment), or by asking the person less threatening, more casual questions such as something relating to interest, hobbies, or demographics. Furthermore, time spent by the group leader with this quiet member outside of the group, one-on-one, building a relationship of trust and friendship, will do much to encourage his or her participation in the group.

The Superficial Person

Another troublesome character in some small groups is the person who specializes in vague generalities. The superficial person avoids depth, fearing change or intimacy and the work and risks involved. Thus this person keeps his or her part of the conversation light, impersonal, and lacking in concreteness. She or he seems to have a "don't rock the boat" attitude and sometimes blend their superficiality with monopolizing the group interaction. While on the surface, at moderate levels this does not seem to be a significant detriment to the group, over the course of many sessions, group apathy, boredom, or frustration can result from the influence of a superficial group member.

One category of superficial group members is that of the perpetual joker or what Satir would describe as the "mascot." These people attract attention to themselves and divert attention from what they perceive, consciously or unconsciously, as uncomfortable, system-threatening situations in the group through an over-abundant use of humor. Early in the group's life this can be useful, for it helps make the group fun and enjoyable. So too, as an occasional comic relief at points throughout the life of the group, humor can help invigorate the group. Yet, as a repetitive, predictable, persistent behavior, it becomes quite disruptive.

While respect for the individual would allow for the person to remain superficial, the leader needs to consider the overall well-being of the group. A confrontation with the effect of the person's superficiality may be helpful both to the individual and to the group as a whole. The skills of concreteness, "alternative frames of reference," "advanced accurate empathy," and delineating action-oriented steps are useful in dealing with a superficial group member.

The Emotional Exposer

Occasionally a group member seems to share more emotion or intimacy than that which would appear to be appropriate for the group at a particular point in the group's life. While catharsis and the experience of intimacy are to be encouraged in most groups (keeping in mind, of course, the purpose of the group), too much too soon or too often interferes with the effective functioning of the group. Such an inappropriate display can frighten the less expressive person or, particularly if repeated frequently by the same person, appear overdone, feigned, and/or artificial. This high level of emotional exposure can turn others off, increasing apathy and boredom toward the group, or build irritation and resentment toward that individual.

Often the emotional "flasher" is looking for attention and approval through shocking others, through doing what people are "supposed" to do in groups, or simply by thrusting their emotions on others. Thus a helpful response is to respond minimally, almost casually, to the excess, not giving it the attention desired. If the problem persists, a gentle, tentative, firm confrontation with the effect of the behavior is most helpful—that is, pointing out your personal discomfort ("immediacy") or the group's discomfort with that person's behavior.

The Sporadic Attendee

A final problem group member is the one who attends the group sporadically and either verbally or nonverbally communicates a lack of commitment to the group. A person attending the group occasionally has a detrimental effect and keeps the group from moving in a more or less direct fashion toward the fulfillment of each stage. A sporadic attendee tends to keep the group at Stage I, for inclusion has not yet been completed for that individual. Each time he or she reappears, there is a need to go back to Stage I and accomplish the inclusion of that occasional member.

There are numerous reasons for a group participant's attending sporadically. He or she may have difficulty forming solid commitments on which to follow through. This inability to make firm commitments may be veiled in a "Joe Cool" attitude that actually seems to express arrogance toward participation. Occasional attendance could also reflect a hidden conflict that a person is experiencing with someone else within the group. It could be a subtle attention-getting device (Have you ever been in a group where the members kept talking about the person who was not there—then showered attention on him or her on the occasions when they returned?). Again, "advanced accurate empathy," "alternative frames of reference," and confrontation with the effect of this behavior is helpful in dealing with this problem member.

Helping a Problem Member

One final word about problem members. There is a need to recognize, support, and affirm the positive behaviors that these problem group members demonstrate in the group. Positive reinforcement has a much greater impact on a person than does criticism. The best way to help a problem member is to encourage and honor those good contributions he or she makes to the group. Of course the same is true for the steady, "normal" group member who is actively contributing to the group's life. The group and each participant benefits from having positive, contributing behavior recognized, encouraged, and reinforced.

GROUP PROCESS PROBLEMS

Not only do difficulties for groups arise from dealing with difficult group members, but they also develop from problems within the process of dynamics of the group. These can occur even in the absence of any of those troublesome folks just described and discussed. Now look at ten potential problems that may develop in the life of a small group.

Entrance of a New Member

When a new person joins an already established group, the group's equilibrium, its homeostasis or balance, is upset and the group must adjust and adapt to this intrusion. How readily the group adapts and forms a new equilibrium will determine how much of a problem (or opportunity!) will be created by the entrance of the new person into the group. Is the group system a closed, rigid one, or is it an open, flexible, and adaptable system? Is it a chaotic system or a stable and secure system?

If the group has difficulty including a new participant, the group will need to deal with this fact about its life. Depending upon the leadership style, the purpose of the group, and the stage of its development, the leader and/or the group will need to work through what is happening to the group as a result of the new member. This, of course, must be done with a sensitivity toward both the needs of the new member and the needs of the continuing members. The presence of this dynamic can be an excellent teaching and learning situation for the members of the group.

New blood can be very stimulating or very disruptive to a group. When a new person joins a group, that group automatically returns to Stage I in its dynamics, and its first primary task is to include the new member. This may seem like a regression to the other members, and indeed it is. Yet the entrance of a new member can stimulate new growth and move the group on to higher levels of development. Ingrown groups can become very narcissistic and ineffective, taking on characteristics of a segregated social club, thus detracting from their prime purpose.

Frustration over the regression to earlier levels of group life can be experienced by the continuing members. They may also feel some fear about breaking up the old familiar patterns that have developed within the group. One useful way of involving the older group members in adjusting to the new members is to ask the continuing members to describe the group and interpret the group norms, purposes, and history to the new person.

Crisis—Hurt Member

A second group dynamic problem that can occur is created by a group member who has experienced a crisis either within the group itself or outside the group and brings the hurt or anxiety of that crisis to the group. A member may announce in a group session something that has happened outside the group that is very traumatic for that person—a job loss, the death of a family member, the report of an accident, or reporting the diagnosis of a serious illness. Because of the relationships that have already developed among the members, the entire group can become emotionally involved. In the midst of a group meeting one participant may get very angry with another member quite suddenly, someone may make a statement that triggers enormous pain and sadness to another, or deep grief can be experienced as someone announces they are leaving the group. What happens to the person and to the group at that moment is crucial to the further life of the group. We have already discussed catharsis, the healthy release of an intense emotion, and its value both to the individual expressing the feelings and to the group itself. As a leader of the group, it is very important that you do not squelch the natural, spontaneous, healthy catharsis but allow the feelings to come forward, supporting the individuals in finding appropriate means for expressing and coping with those feelings. The crisis and the hurt should not be ignored. A leader would do well to reach out in warmth, understanding, love, and acceptance.

Self-centered, Ingrown Groups

Some groups that have met together over a long period of time can become very ingrown and focused entirely upon themselves. Some of these groups can continue to exist for long periods of time and become essentially social clubs that

have as an objective (although usually unstated) the mainte-
nance of the social relationships within the group. As goal-
oriented small groups they eventually lose their functions.
In the process, the primary or original goals for which the
group was formed may be lost. As the awareness of this situation dawns (often it is preceded by a growing or lingering
sense of apathy) it is wise for the group to assess its current
situation, redefine its purpose, formally conclude, or else move
on to Stage III.

Power Subgroup

Sometimes within a group that is a little too large or a group
in which there is a conflict over the leadership of the group
(particularly when the stated leader is not the natural leader)
a power subgroup is formed within the larger group. Often
a power struggle emerges in that situation, leaving other members of the group feeling excluded. When this develops it is
important that the leader and the group deal openly with
this factor, confronting again the effects of this dynamic on
the group as a whole. If the group is an advanced group and
well into Stage II, it would be very appropriate for the entire
group to struggle through what has happened as a result of
the formation of this small power clique. As this factor is dealt
with, a reminder or a re-definition of the purpose of the group
should be offered; some discussion of the group's stage, process, and direction would help the group work through this
problem. The persistence of a small power group over many
sessions, will eventually erode the effectiveness and desirability of the group for its members.

Inappropriate Setting

Some groups suffer because the location for the group meetings is inappropriate to their purpose and effective functioning. Imagine, for instance, an intensive therapy group trying
to function effectively in a lobby of a college student union
or in a small, crowded office around a messy cluttered
desk. Consider the impact of its setting when a task-oriented

group meets next to a picture window that looks out on a playground crowded with screaming, laughing children, or in a hotel dining room with a rock band playing loudly a few feet away. A setting inappropriate for the particular purpose of a group can create problems in the effectiveness of that group.

Conflict of Goals

Another group process problem that can emerge at any point in a group's life, but particularly at the earlier stages, is that of a conflict over goals. Many times the purpose or goals of the leader are in conflict with the goals, needs, or expectations of the participants. The question that has to be addressed when this occurs is whose agenda will take priority, the group's or the leader's? This can be either a highly disruptive problem or a great opportunity to develop into a more dynamic and potent group, depending on the nondefensiveness and strength of the leader and on the willingness of the participants to work together to form a shared agenda based on shared expectations and goals. There is at work at this point in a group's life, the need for a collaborative style of work. A dynamic mix of leader and group goals can emerge and lead to more profound effectiveness for the group.

Awkward Relationships Between Members

A wide range of interpersonal relationships can develop within a small group, particularly in a group that meets together over a long period of time. We have already discussed the tendency of a small group to recreate the families of origin for each of the participants. This can happen in a rather benign, calm, orderly, flexible fashion; on the other hand, it can become rigid, painful, and conflict producing with the potential for disastrous consequences to the group. Add to that the element of transference occurring, creating group mothers, fathers, favorite little sons, or charming, flirtatious daughters. A more obvious difficulty is the emergence of romantic attractions that often develop in the life of a small group. All of these awkward relationships create strained dynamics in the life of the group. Usually (especially if the group is well into the second stage of its development) it is most helpful to deal with these relationships openly and directly. At times it may not be possible or advantageous to face these relationships openly within the group. In that event, the leader should certainly note and perhaps discuss the impact of those relationships upon the group privately with those involved, particularly if it is interfering with the group's effectiveness.

Group Superficiality

If the group seems to be unproductive and superficial in its impact or ineffective in meeting its purpose, the group would benefit from discussion of this superficiality together as a whole group. This is particularly true for the older, more established group. I have indicated earlier that conflict between participants in a group will often be reflected in group apathy or boredom because the members avoid facing the conflict directly. In so doing, they unconsciously allow their irritation and resentments to cause them to withdraw emotionally from the same active involvement with the group that they previously had. Another source of the superficiality may be the conflict between leader goals and group goals as previously discussed. If there is a relative balance of power between the group and the leader, this conflict over goals, if undiagnosed, may result in a standoff that makes productivity very difficult. Perhaps there are other group, leader, or participant problems and they should be investigated.

Bringing a consultant or a co-leader into the group at this point might be very helpful. Another person, as an outsider to the established system, may be able through more objective observation to spot a conflict or missing ingredient that has gone undiagnosed by both the leader and the group. Perhaps group superficiality should signal to the established group the readiness to terminate or move on to Stage III. On the other hand, perhaps the stagnation of the group at a particular point is simply a "seasonal slump" that will resolve itself. It is hard, if not impossible, for a group to have steady productivity over a long period of time. Ups and downs are normative to most groups.

Going Too Deep Too Soon

Just as an individual can reveal too much emotion or intimacy too soon or in an inappropriate manner, so too can an entire group. Instant intimacy and immediate in-depth relationships rarely, if ever, occur. It takes time to build relationships that have depth and closeness; yet some groups attempt to create this intimacy too quickly without allowing the necessary time to build those relationships. When this happens it is important for the skilled leader to clarify the purpose of the group with the members. Furthermore, the group, at the leader's direction, can observe process and communicate the effect of those inappropriate emotional expressions on the group's life.

Conversations and personal disclosures occur with varying degrees of personal threat. The sharing of ideas, information, and theories is less threatening than the reporting of personal experiences out of the past. Communicating about personal problems and feelings outside the group increases the intensity of potential threat to a group participant. Talking about the "here and now" relationships within the group is even more threatening. The greatest threat is that of sharing personal items not usually discussed with anyone other than a family member, one's most intimate and trusted friend, or a professional. The more threatening the topic of conversation is, the less appropriate it is for a Stage I group and the more appropriate it is for Stages II through IV (especially Stage II). Talking about "here and now" relationships within the group and the disclosure of one's most intimate thoughts, feelings, and desires is too threatening for the Stage I group and tends to exclude rather than include the more timid participant. Yet at Stage II these more threatening topics are important to the maturity of that group. Throughout a group's life the strength, skill, and maturity of leadership, as well as the purpose of the group, effects what the appropriate level of emotional expression and interpersonal intimacy is at that point in the group's development.

As indicated elsewhere, apathy, boredom, and dullness in a group may suggest hidden conflict within the group. A small group of which I was a member had met together for two or three years for the purpose of emotional support and mutual challenge to growth. It had been a highly satisfying experience for all six of us and it was quite surprising to each of us to find that our group was in a slump that went beyond a seasonal slump. Interest lagged, attendance became sporadic, and we struggled to find what was causing the disruption. Finally in one session it surfaced—two of the men, close personal friends outside of the group, felt a deep conflict that had never surfaced and been articulated. As it did surface and was articulated (and it was a tense, painful catharsis), energy came to the surface, and the group rallied both to the two persons who were openly discussing their conflict and to the group as a whole. The open expression of conflict that had been hidden brought new enthusiasm to the group.

Sometimes when a group is suffering from dullness and apathy the occasional and limited use of humor, joking, and/ or small talk can help break the group out of its doldrums. A brief moment of laughter in a lethargic session can sometimes lift the energy level of the group and free the group for greater intensity. At times, with clear understanding of what she or he is doing, the leader can play the role of devil's advocate and create controversy for the sake of injecting new life into the group. Once again, caution is important in using either of these strategies so as not to divert the group away from its primary task. When a group persists in apathy and dullness and there is no hidden conflict within the group, it may be time to move on to Stage III or to conclude.

Member Leaving

Just as the entrance of a new member into the group necessarily affects the group process, so too the leaving of a group member can have a profound effect on the group's life. A member can leave a group before the group terminates because of external necessities, because they have received what they wanted to gain from the group, or as a way of avoiding conflict and/or intimacy. Whatever the reason for leaving, it is good to formalize the leave-taking; allowing good-bye's to be said and the grief process to run its course and be experienced by each of the group members. The next few sessions will reflect some of the mourning that the individuals feel over the absent person. Yet if the leaving is handled in a straightforward, relatively formal manner (rather than the person simply not showing up again) the adjustment to the loss and change of group composition can occur in the most helpful and least disruptive way.

Developmental Stage Incomplete

Another group dynamic problem that can, and frequently does, occur is that of moving to the next developmental stage prematurely, before the current or preceding stage is finished. If a group is experiencing difficulty in Stage II, "Work: Understanding and Growth," perhaps Stage I, "Inclusion and Exploration," has not been sufficiently completed. While I have said that in a developmental framework Stage I is present in Stage II, nevertheless, a sufficient level of completion needs to have occurred in one stage before the group is ready to move on. It is hard to accomplish growth and change if the members of the group still do not feel included in the group.

LEADERSHIP PROBLEMS

Group problems can also develop out of leadership problems other than those that are caused by lack of the leadership skills that are listed under each of the three stages in this book. There are two additional leadership issues that need to be discussed at this point. As discussed earlier, if the appointed or elected leader is also the natural leader the leadership function will be carried out in the most productive manner. On the other hand, if the natural leader is not the appointed leader, important obstacles are placed in the way of the group's effectiveness. Thus, I will discuss the problems that arise out of group leadership as well as the specific steps that a group leader can take to develop natural leadership.

Power Struggle

Power struggles frequently occur within the life of a small group, whether between an appointed leader and a natural leader, two co-leaders, or two or more natural leaders. As in any power struggle this can have either disastrous or highly creative results.

The longer a group continues to meet, the more likely it becomes that a natural leader will emerge. The ideal situation occurs when the appointed leader happens to be the natural leader. Fortunately this occurs with some frequency. However, the natural leader is often someone else from within the group. When this happens there is the potential for, if not the experience of, a power struggle. Power struggles can also occur between the stated or appointed leader and a competitive challenger, who may or may not be the natural leader but who chooses to compete for the leadership of the group. Sometimes the group informally chooses one of its members as a spokesperson who then may become involved in a power struggle with the appointed leader.

When these power struggles develop it is very important that the appointed leader not be overly threatened by this challenge. If he or she can avoid being defensive and keep from getting caught in a competitive match, the appointed leader will minimize the competitive challenge, remain in control of himself or herself and the group, and reflect natural leadership qualities. If possible, the appointed leader should make a useful ally out of the natural leader and gently enlist her or his help in the effective functioning of the group. All of the leadership skills we have discussed so far are important for the group leader to develop and utilize when facing a challenge to his or her leadership (accurate empathy [both primary and advanced], respect, concreteness, "alternative frames of reference," confrontation, self-disclosure, etc.).

While the transfer of leadership to the group itself may be very appropriate and useful in the later phases (Stage III and the second half of Stage II) of a group's development, it is disastrous for the beginning group. An exception to this is where there is a highly self-motivated, highly skilled group of peers that can rotate, share, and monitor the internal leadership of the group. If a leader finds himself or herself inclined to be timid and to give up the leadership function (except to initiate the group process), it is important for that leader to take a risk, leap into the leadership role, and "act as if." To that leader's great surprise she or he may (and probably will) soon be functioning as a leader. Much of leadership is simply assuming and taking leadership—deciding to lead and leading.

Leader Dominates

The opposite group problem, of course, is the situation when the leader dominates and is unwilling to give up the leadership when, for the group's purpose and effective functioning, it

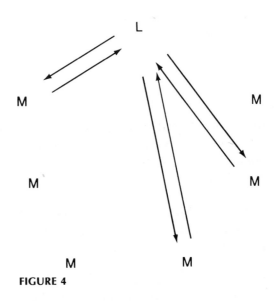

FIGURE 4

should appropriately be transferred to the group. The leader (and it is often the novice, insecure leader) who tenaciously holds onto leadership, dominates the interaction, centers the group around the leader, limits the interaction among the group members, and dramatically reduces the dynamic potential of the group. In a group where all conversation is directed to or through the leader, there is a limited and constricted dynamic, as reflected in this diagram.

Compare the dynamic of the group in Figure 4 with the following:

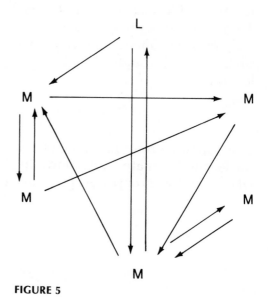

FIGURE 5

In Figure 5, the leader shares the group process with the other members of the group, which opens up many more possibilities and provides far greater energy for the group experience.

Seven Steps to Natural Leadership. Ernest and Nancy Bormann, list these seven steps which I have included to help you be a natural as well as a skilled leader.

1. Do not be a manipulator.
2. Be willing to pay the price; leadership is hard work.

3. Talk up—take an active interest in each participant.
4. Do your homework (yet do not be overly compulsive).
5. Make personal sacrifices.
6. Raise the status of the group members.
7. Build group cohesiveness.[1]

In short, be a skilled, loving servant to the members of the group, responding to their needs and hopes.

REMEMBER

As you work with and through the problems of a group, remember that the problems can either destroy the group *or* be opportunities for renewal, growth, and new dimensions of group effectiveness and accomplishment. As these problems are confronted and dealt with, the dual attitudes of kindness and encouragement are not only needed but they will also make a significant difference in overcoming the problems (i.e., turning them from obstacles into opportunities). The problems need to be solved with considerable kindness and encouragement. Then, and only then, the group is ready to move on to challenge and Stage III.

ACTIVE LEARNING EXERCISES FOR CHAPTER FOUR

(1) In a practice small group, have one participant function as the practice leader while two other participants role play two of the problem group members discussed in this chapter. The other participants "play it straight," responding naturally. Rotate the roles until each person has had the opportunity of functioning as a practice leader and as one or two problem group members. Incidentally, it would be good for the group to caucus and assign the roles without the practice leader's knowledge.

A current topic of importance to the group members

---

[1] Bormann, Ernest G., and Bormann, Nancy C., *Effective Small Group Communication*. (Minneapolis; Burgess Publishing Co., 1972), pp. 57–59.

should be discussed during this exercise. For example, the group members could discuss the problems they each experience in leading or participating in this or other small groups or the ways in which they have transferred learning from this practice small group into their behaviors outside the group.

As a group, discuss the impact of each problem group member on the group and on the leader. Discuss the effect of the leader's interaction with the problem group members and its impact on those group members individually and on the group as a whole (e.g., What helped and what hindered the effectiveness of the leader in the group?). Use all of the leadership skills that have been presented as you discuss the role play. Presumably, your practice group is now a Stage-II group.

(2) Repeat the above process, role playing one of the group process problems and rotating the leadership role. Again, use a topic of current importance to the group members and debrief the role play by discussing the effect of both the problem and the leadership interventions on the effectiveness of the group. It is very helpful in the debriefing to document your evaluation with what you saw and/or heard that leads you to that conclusion.

(3) Repeat the above process, this time with the leader role playing one of the leadership problems discussed in this chapter. Rotate the leadership role while the remaining group members try to be as natural as possible. The leader should not disclose what he or she is role playing prior to the practice session.

It is useful to discuss something current and personal for the group members. Once again, debrief the role play experience, observing the effects of the leaders' and group members' behaviors on the group as a whole.

chapter five

Stages III and IV—
Challenge: Action and
Completion

Most groups end somewhere in Stage II. Perhaps the time period designated for the group has been completed or the group was designed to be a Stage II group, and when those goals were reached there was a mutual decision to end. Too often, however, a group that began with a strong commitment and sustained an enthusiasm for a considerable length of time, slowly but surely runs out of energy and attractiveness to the participants. The group dies a slow, steady death to the dismay and concern of its members. Attempts to revive the group are short-lived and the dying process continues. Rarely does a group move on and develop through Stage III to a satisfying conclusion in Stage IV. Yet, this further development may be precisely what the struggling, formerly successful group needs to pump vital new life into the group and lead it to a sense of purpose that far transcends its previous purpose. Stage III may provide the golden opportunity for other groups that otherwise finish with Stage II and miss fulfilling its potential, or, for those that seem to finish abruptly, Stage IV could provide a way to bring the group to a close with a sense of accomplishment and gratitude.

Stage III is a major stage in the development of a group. In many instances, it is the purpose for which the group came into being—to effect a change or to instigate positive action. Stage IV is also a major stage although usually brief and to the point. How many times have you been a part of a group that ended with a feeling of incompleteness? The group just seemed to "pass away"; it stopped meeting with no sense of completion, closure, or evaluation. Effective termination and evaluation are an important aspect of a small group's life that is rarely recognized and provided for.

GROUP DYNAMICS—STAGE III

Group Goals

The group goals of this third and final stage of a group's life are action, support, and evaluation. An effectively functioning small group will (or should) eventually lead its participants individually, or as a group, to some sort of action. What the particular action is will depend on the nature and purpose of the group and the learning, growth, and change that takes place in the individual members. The action might be a shared group project, for example, putting on a workshop for the public on a topic of mutual concern, sponsoring a refugee family, or working with the school or corporate administrative staff to change a policy that hinders the well-being of students or employees. Or, this action could be individual, for example, going through the career evaluation and transition process to secure a new job, changing one's living situation by moving from a private home to a townhouse or condominium, or relating differently to one's family expectations for the holidays by going out for dinner rather than going through the intense pressure of cooking the dinner at home. Whatever the particular action is, taking positive action is important for the participants of a small group no matter what the group's purpose is. The understanding and growth that occurs in Stage II needs to translate into some form of action in order for it to be valid and useful.

Throughout the action phase, the group needs to be very supportive of one another. Action, especially new action, activity reflecting change, is usually difficult. Our personal inertia wants to keep us from taking big steps. It is often risky and scary. We resist change and find that the movements we make come slowly and (at times) painfully. Critical to staying with the task and taking action on new learning is the steady support of others. Therefore, support giving is an important goal of Stage III.

Evaluation by the group members of themselves and of the group as a whole is also very important to the life of a small group. It is useful both near the end of the group's life and also periodically throughout the life of the group to make careful evaluations of the group process, effectiveness, and value to the members. Is the group developing, and is it achieving its goals? What helped and what hindered the successful goal accomplishment of the group? What can be learned from the group that can be transferred to life generally, to the specific concerns of the individuals, to future groups, and so on?

Helpful Group Dynamics

An important dynamic that needs to be recognized about Stage III groups is that this is a comprehensive stage. That is to say, the dynamics of a third stage group include all of the dynamics of Stages I and II, and builds on them. Thus, in order to fulfill this stage, all of the dynamics of the previous stages are and need to be operating in this stage. Furthermore, all of the skills of each of the three stages need to be exercised. Thus, it is important that the leader of a Stage III group, as she or he considers the particular dynamics and skills involved in Stage III, recognize the presence of all of the other group dynamics and skills from the previous stages. Not only are there new dynamics at this level, the previous dynamics discussed in Chapters Two and Three are also present: the resolution of housekeeping details, providing information, socializing, genuine concern, common experience, emotional expression, the informal formation of rules and norms, atmosphere of hope, cohesiveness, creation of family, learning from each other, initiating transition and change, and evaluation. To these we add the particular dynamics of Stage III.

Cooperation. Cooperation is the first important Stage III group dynamic that we encounter and need to facilitate as leaders. If the group has been functioning effectively, the participant has been learning cooperation all through Stages I and II. As the group moves into Stage III, cooperation is a necessity. Since any action that the group will take (and even most individual action) is a collaborative effort, the group member must actively involve himself or herself in the planning and execution of that action. The effective group functions as a team, working together to accomplish their shared mutual task. No longer is each person simply an independent individual focusing on or concerned with personal concerns, rather, the members are working together for the common goals. In so doing, they are learning how to give to, respond to, and participate with each other cooperatively.

Subgrouping. A second dynamic that can occur at any level of a group's life, but that has particular significance at Stage III, is that of subgrouping. The forming of smaller groups within a group may suggest that the group is too large to function at maximum effectiveness or that cohesiveness and cooperation have not been fully developed. Just when the group ought to be ready to "make its move" in taking positive action, a subgroup can form and seriously disrupt the process with negative consequences both for those who are included in the subgroup as well as those who are excluded. Continuous team building is important all the way through the life of the group, including the action stage.

Conflict Among Members. While it can develop at any stage, conflict in Stage III can develop over whose goals and priorities will be adopted by the group. Also, dependency and independency issues can emerge in the form of a conflict over who takes the lead and whether or not a participant will cooperate with that other person's leadership. These conflicts need to be dealt with openly as soon as possible so that attention can be given to and not diverted from the action task. If Stage II has been effective, the group should be able to resolve these issues rather quickly. Otherwise, some return to Stage II work may be necessary before giving full attention to the tasks of Stage III.

Risk Taking.　A fourth dynamic important to Stage III is the capacity for individuals and the group to take *risks.* Each member of the group needs to realize the importance of taking creative, healthy risks. Risk taking is part of growth and change. It is part of life. To live and to grow is to risk leaving the old familiar and safe places and venture forth into the new and unknown with no absolute certainties of success and accomplishment.

Richard Leider, coauthor of *The Inventurers,*[1] in a lecture on job transition, defined four types of risk takers: those who avoid taking risks, those who are given a basic core of risks that come from their life settings, those who are excitement seekers, and those who are "Inventurers." "Inventurers" is a word coined in the book by that name to refer to those who adventure inward and actively, thoughtfully, and creatively form and take their own risks. To creatively and courageously form and take good, healthy risks requires relationships of trust in others who can guide, guard, and support the risk taking. It requires the dual functions of cooperation and support by the other group members to provide a conducive environment for risk taking. Taking risks in this context of group care, support, and skill (i.e., trust) is thereby thoughtful and not careless or reckless. However, to take the step, to put new thought into new action, no matter how reasonable and well thought out, is still a risk.

Often there are group members who find risk taking difficult because of fear or inexperience, or because the step is an unusually large step. For them, a process of systematically increasing the level of risk can be helpful and reassuring. By starting with small risks, the person or group can systemati-

---

[1] Richard Leider and Janet Hagberg, *The Inventurers* (Reading, Massachusetts: Addison-Wesley, 1978).

cally work up to more difficult, threatening, or complex risks until the big step is taken. It has been said that the only way one can eat an elephant, is one bite at a time. As the small risks are taken, and then the increasingly difficult steps are risked, positive reinforcement is crucial. Rewarding even the small successes and comforting the failures or setbacks make an important contribution to the achievement of the major risk-taking step.

Action Taking. The capacity to *take action* is the next important factor in Stage III both for the individual group members and for the group as a whole. Action taking can be both positive—the starting or doing of something—or negative—the stopping or ending of something. Also, action taking can be personal, subgroup, or whole group action. The crucial aspect being the willingness to initiate and the capacity to follow through on the action taken.

Useful for action taking by either an individual or the group is the skill of goal setting. Defining and establishing clear, concrete, workable, reasonable, measurable, and desirable goals is the first step to effective action. Notice especially the words "concrete," "workable," and "desirable." Each is important in translating dreams and hopes into action that can and will occur. People fail to act on goals when they are either vague and general, unrealistic, grandiose, impossible, or undesirable.

Once the goal has been established, the individual or group should list and organize action programs that are needed to accomplish the goal. A realistic, systematic action plan will facilitate action on the part of the person or group. Priority assignment is an important step to taking positive action. Often people are discouraged from taking action by being overwhelmed with the number of action steps that are possible and desirable. In some instances, a person or group can become paralyzed by all the possibilities and thus unable to respond to any alternative. By putting the steps in order of priority, a person can gain a better understanding of where to start. Thus, that person will have a feeling of accomplishment knowing that even if only a couple of steps are taken, something has been accomplished. Even taking a few small steps is more desirable than passively observing and doing nothing.

Reality testing is also useful for effective action taking. Having an awareness of what is possible and realistic, and knowing what does and does not work, is very helpful in stimulating action taking.

Then one simply needs to implement the action program. While the implementation part of the process is occurring and after it is over, the evaluation of the action program is an important and usually ignored step in the process. Throughout the carrying out of the action plan, goal setting, "prioritizing," and reality testing, evaluating what worked and what didn't work insures the success of the action program.

Reflection, Evaluation and Reinforcement. Systematic reflection and evaluation and the reinforcement of successful action taking is important to a third-level group. Observing and reflecting on what did or did not happen, and how it happened or didn't happen, increases learning. Most of us learn much from observing what we do and then reflecting on it. The reinforcement underscores and helps ingrain and integrate the learning. In addition, it helps make the learning process enjoyable and, therefore, increases the desirability of continuing or repeating the process. Positive reinforcement encourages participation in the process and the success of the action taking. Incidentally, success and reinforcement for the success should be seen more in relationship to having taken action than in the actual outcome of the action. The individual or the group does have control over and is responsible for the taking of action, but not for the outcome of that action. It is the doing more than the result of the doing (except for consideration in the evaluation process) that needs to be rewarded. Even action that has not produced the desired result can be very positive and beneficial for the individual or the group.

Leadership Goals

The leader's primary responsibility in Stage III is to facilitate the action program to which the group and the individuals are committed to offer skilled support, and to bring about a clear, effective completion to the group's task. As such, she or he needs the skills of facilitating, elaborating action programs, supportive counseling, and the capacity to clearly focus personal and group responsibility.

Leadership Skills

Facilitator. The skilled small group leader working with a third stage group needs to be a facilitating or enabling leader. At Stage III, most of the content responsibility and group leadership has shifted to the group itself.

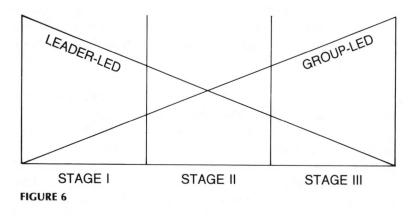

STAGE I   STAGE II   STAGE III

FIGURE 6

Yet, the leader still has important leadership functions, although now it is more behind the scenes—encouraging, challenging, supporting, clarifying, that is, facilitating. As the facilitator effectively stimulates and guides the group through the steps of action, he or she becomes an enabler of the resources, skills, and leadership functions within the group, allowing them to emerge and govern its future life. If he or she has been an effective leader to this point, the leadership that emerges will be more or less modeled after that of the leader; his or her style will prevail. However, the energy and responsibility for leading will be with the group. The skilled leader has enabled the group to effectively assume these tasks.

Develop Action Plans. As an enabler or facilitator of the group's resources and action plan, the skilled leader will need to be able to stimulate the development of several plans of action. One person, or the group as a whole, will become aware of the need to take action in some area, yet help is often needed in knowing how to take that step. The leader is usually expected to be able to skillfully lead them in the forming of action steps. The leader knows and keeps before her or him the purpose, task, or function of the group. Why is the group in existence, and what is its charter? Furthermore, it is important for the leader to be able to effect a collaborative decision regarding the individual and/or shared tasks. The more the group and its members "own" the task, the more they will invest themselves in its accomplishment. The action decision needs to belong to the group and its members, not to the leader. Hopefully, it will be a mutually satisfying decision. It is very helpful to the group's work at Stage III to have the leader enable the group or individuals to list their alternative goals and choices and to select the most appropriate and desirable goal from the several alternatives. Keep in mind that the selection belongs to the group and should not be forced or manipulated upon them by the leader (keeping in mind, of course, the particular purpose for which the group was formed).

Gerard Egan describes a seven step field-force approach to the establishment of workable action programs:

1. Identify and clarify the problem.
2. Establish priorities.
3. Establish workable goals.
4. Tally available resources.
5. Choose the means.

6. Establish criteria for evaluation.
7. Implementation.[2]

First, the group (or the individual) identifies and clarifies the problems, needs, and opportunities that exist. These should be stated concretely in a way that makes the problem appear solvable. As we said earlier, an effective goal and/or action plan needs to be conceivable, desirable, workable, measurable, and realistic, that is, it can be accomplished! It is important for the group to "own" the problem from the start, that is, it is a problem or need that the members believe they have and which they want to do something or have something done to meet that need or solve that problem. They will not "own" the work involved in achieving the goal if they do not think they "own" the problem. Once the problem or need has been identified, clarified, and stated concretely, the issue should then be broken down into smaller, more workable, and manageable units. Again, how do you eat an elephant? One bite at a time! Individually, or together as a group, people have little control over general outcomes, but we have great control over whether or not we work on the pieces.

Second, the leader needs to have the ability to establish priorities in choosing the unit or issue to work on. People (including small groups and inexperienced group leaders) often have a tendency to try to solve many problems or satisfy several needs all at once. They are like hunters who want to fire a huge shotgun and hit everything in sight, real or imagined! However, when hunting a large, strong animal, one well-aimed rifle shot is usually more effective than a shotgun blast. So too, huge, multifaceted problems are better faced and confronted with one well-placed action step than trying to solve the entire issue at once. An elephant is eaten by taking one bite at a time—not by swallowing the entire elephant!

In selecting the bite to eat or the place at which to aim the rifle, it is useful to choose that problem (or those problems)

[2] Egan, *The Skilled Helper*, pp. 200–229. The leader would do well to know these seven steps for goal setting and action planning to use in facilitating the group's action steps.

which is under one's control, that is, a problem about which something can be done. Remember, we cannot change other people, only ourselves. Top priority should be given to the crisis or most pressing issue. It is here that a person's attention is focused anyhow, and the more severe the crisis, the less able one is to deal effectively with other concerns. Egan suggests further that priority be given to that which can be handled relatively easily. Successfully completing action on an easy task usually builds confidence and excitement for tackling bigger and more complex issues. At times, however, those large, difficult issues are so crucial that if they can be accomplished, the other issues fall into place with relative ease, and even if they don't, at least the big issue has been dealt with, and hopefully, action taken towards its resolution. Another principle Egan suggests for establishing priorities is to give priority to that which is likely to have a general impact— the "ripple effect." Successful action on a general concern, like a stone dropping into the water producing ever-enlarging rings or ripples reaching out away from the point of impact, will have positive impact in a wide range of areas.

Third, the leader needs to be able to facilitate the establishing of workable goals. The goals as we have said, need to be stated concretely in a way that makes them workable and achievable. Grandiose goals stated vaguely produce frustration and despair, and thus become counterproductive. A goal can be set too high. Also, it is important that the selected goal is indeed the group's goal and not the leader's goal. The group (or individual) needs to "own" the goal as their own goal. Whatever goal is selected needs to be broken down into workable parts which become "minigoals."

Fourth, the group needs to take a census of the resources available. This begins with a listing of those forces that will (or could) hinder or interfere with the achievement of the goal. We need to be aware and realistic about the situation, noting that which can sabotage success. Then, there is a need to list those resources that are required to achieve the goal and which are available to the group, both from within and from outside the group. It may be helpful to underline those that seem the most important and accessible. After this inventory has taken place, the group (or the individual) can list all of the possible action steps that could be employed to reach the goal.

Fifth, the group can then choose the means that will most effectively achieve the established goals. Incidentally, Egan emphasizes the importance of making certain that the means chosen are in keeping with the individual's and the group's values. The effective, facilitating leader can help the group members choose those programs that have the highest probability for success (future effort is positively correlated to present or past success). Egan describes four strategies for choosing action programs.[3] The first is what he calls the "wish" strategy—choosing action programs that could achieve the goals if resources and skills are unlimited. The "safe" strategy is employed by those who want to take no risks and be absolutely certain of a positive outcome. Some choose the "escape" strategy which enables the person to avoid the worst possible outcome. A fourth, and desired strategy, is the "combination" strategy. Here a person tries to minimize the danger while maximizing the benefit that could come from such a plan of action and the probability of its success. Throughout the selection of action plans, the leader would do well to help the individual or group move step by step toward the goal. In a hospital lobby, I noted a slogan emphasizing that we accomplish big tasks by persistently taking small steps—a "winning by inches" approach. The slogan read: "Mile by mile, life is a trial. Yard by yard, life is hard. Inch by inch, it's a cinch!"

Sixth, the leader can help facilitate the group's action programs by enabling it to establish criteria for measuring the effectiveness of its action plan. Is there some way of objectifying the assessment or the evaluation of the program? How can we measure what is being accomplished and the effectiveness of the current plans of action?

Seventh, the leader needs to facilitate the implementation of the action program. The individual member or the group as a whole needs to put into effect the means chosen for achieving the established goals. A time comes when discus-

[3] Egan, *The Skilled Helper*, pp. 222–223.

sion ceases and action begins, and the leader can encourage, challenge, and, at times, push for that action, recognizing of course that the decision to act and the action itself needs to be "owned" by the group or group member. Throughout the implementation phase, the skills of Stages I and II need to be utilized, remembering that Stage III builds upon and carries with it, the first two stages.

In addition to the seven steps Egan lists, there are three additional steps that are useful:

8. Positive reward.
9. Report in and evaluate.
10. Celebrate.

The eighth is the use of positive reinforcement as an important tool for the facilitative leader. Reward for positive effort and achievement is highly motivating to the person who is attempting new behavior, or for the group that is attempting a new program. With reward accomplishment, there is greater likelihood that the person or group will continue taking action and engage in similar new programs in the future. Criticism or punishment usually does little to stimulate success or to avoid future failure. In fact, it usually encourages failure. The same is true for the leader's avoidance of the unsuccessful person or group which is often experienced as a passive punishment by that leader.

Ninth, the effective leader should facilitate an opportunity for the participants to report in on the work they have done in carrying out their action program(s). The focus of such a "report-in" session should be on collecting objective data, that is, measuring the goal and action program achievement by previously designed measurements. Furthermore, it should provide an opportunity for each person to "unload" his or her feelings, reactions, and reflections in a spirit of support that allows for catharsis and objective evaluation. This does not need to be a lengthy philosophical review of all that has gone into establishing these particular goals and action plans, but a time to release emotions and evaluate objectively one's progress in the program.

If the program has achieved its goal, how did it do so, how was success accomplished, and what can be learned from this experience that can be transferred to new goals and new action programs? If the program has failed, where did the program fall apart or fail? Was the goal inappropriate because it was unworkable, unrealistic, or undesirable? Was the action program insufficient to accomplish its objective? What can be changed for the next try, that is, what change can be made in the action program? Notice the focus for evaluating both success and failure is not on *why*, but *what*. The evaluation should not be a philosophical discussion of "whys" nor criticism which places the person on the defensive. Rather, the leader's or group's evaluation should be factually and objectively oriented while remaining personally open, kind, and supportive.

Tenth, when action has taken place, whether it was met with huge success or failure, celebration of the action taken can be facilitated by the leader. In most instances, the work of the group leader is to lead the group as a whole, or individually, to positive action. As we have indicated earlier, outcomes are usually out of the control of the individual, particularly the group leader. While we hope and work for positive outcomes, it is the taking of positive action that is the crucial focal point of the group's life. That positive action step should be celebrated. Then, after the celebration and the group's work is finished, it is time for the group leader to enable the group to conclude.

Provide Support.   A critical group leader's skill throughout this third stage is that of providing *support.* Supportive counseling has been defined by Howard Clinebell as that which helps stabilize, undergird, nurture, motivate, or guide an individual, and which encourages the individual to utilize the resources that he or she has toward the resolution of that person's own needs.[4] This primarily involves listening (attending and primary empathy, as described in Stage I) and then positive encouragement to continue drawing from the participant's own resources. Being skillfully supportive means the

---

[4] Howard Clinebell, *Basic Types of Pastoral Counseling* (Nashville: Abingdon, 1966), pp. 139–140.

leader must not "rescue" the struggling group member, doing that individual's work for him or her. As eager as the leader may be to have successful outcomes to the action program(s) the group members are involved in, she or he must avoid leaping in and making it successful for them. Likewise, the effective leader needs to refrain from keeping group members from making a mistake. Respect and support allows the participants to make their own mistakes and victories and to learn from them. The supportive leader is there, "with" them, when they report about the experiences they have had as they implemented their action programs. The effective supportive leader allows for a catharsis, offers encouragement, and facilitates an objective evaluation, while respecting the autonomy and the capacities of each individual and of the group as a whole.

Keep the Focus of Responsibility Clear. A related skill that is important at this stage (as indeed it is at each stage), but in a different way, is that of being able to maintain a clear focus of responsibility. It is important for the well-being of everyone concerned—the group as a whole, each individual, and the leader (or at least the group leader)—to know where the lines of responsibility need to be drawn. The leader should keep in mind the question "Where does ownership or responsibility for the problem, the task, or the program lie?" "Whose problem is it?" "Whose task is the group or individual trying to accomplish?" "Whose program is it?" Clear responsibility boundaries need to be drawn so that the leader does not become overly responsible for the well-being of each member or of the group itself, and become personally emeshed in problems that are not the leader's. Nor should the effective leader be "underresponsible," detached, and isolated from the needs and concerns of the group. His or her responsibility is for the effective leading and facilitating of the group, and thus the effectiveness of the group in stimulating positive group or individual outcomes. The leader would do well to "let go" of taking responsibility for others, yet share a warm, genuine, and deep concern for what happens in and through the group to each individual, as well as to the group, and responsibly offer his or her skills to the disposal of the members.[5] Keeping the focus of responsibility clear and helping others to do so as well, is an important skill in leading a small group.

Evaluating. An evaluation, not only of the action programs, but of the entire group process, is very useful. In fact, it is essential for discovering what you are accomplishing or have accomplished over the life of the group. Feedback is essential for learning what worked and what didn't, and how to improve your leadership or group experience in the future. Here the group leader again takes the initiative in order to facilitate this important process. The following is one sample form for such an evaluation:[6]

> What do you feel about this group? *(first words that come to mind)*
> In this group, the most helpful aspects were _____
> I think the group could be improved by _____
> The least helpful aspect of the group was _____
> In future groups, I hope that _____

GROUP DYNAMICS—STAGE IV

Group Goal

The goal of the fourth and final stage of a group's life is a clear and satisfying termination. Having evaluated the group and recognized that the time has come to end the group, a formal termination is very valuable. Participants need a sense of completion to a group experience which allows them to

---

[5] A simple yet profound communication skill called "speaking for self" is very helpful in keeping lines of responsibility clearly drawn. By making "I" statements, the leader and the members can talk about what they are responsible for—namely their own experiences, thoughts, feelings, desires, and actions—without speaking for others ("you," "we"), and thus becoming overly responsible for them or speaking for no one ("it," "they," "some," "one") and being underresponsible. For outstanding resources in effective interpersonal communication, see Miller, Nunnally, and Wackman, *Talking Together I* (1979), *Alive and Aware* (1975) (Minneapolis: Interpersonal Communication Programs, Inc.) or Miller, Nunnally, Wackman, and Saline, *Straight Talk* (New York: Rawson-Wade Publishers, Inc., 1981).

[6] See the appendix for additional forms.

know both the reality of the ending and a chance to celebrate and/or mourn the completion or conclusion of the group. Rarely does this happen. Usually groups just stop and participants drift away from the group and on to other experiences. In so doing, group members miss both the sense of completing something worthwhile with the atmosphere of celebration and the opportunity to grieve the ending in a ritualized or formal way (only to have that grief transferred to other situations).

Helpful Group Dynamics

Understanding small groups from a developmental perspective asserts that all of the dynamics operative in Stages I through III are operative in a Stage IV or concluding group. Thus, the resolution of housekeeping details, providing information, socializing, genuine concern, common experience, emotional expression, informal formation of rules and norms, atmosphere of hope, cohesiveness, creation of family, learning from each other, initiating transition and change, evaluation, cooperation, subgrouping, intragroup conflict, risk taking, action taking, reflection, evaluation, and reinforcement are all operating within the group as it approaches and actualizes its termination. One additional dynamic is introduced now at Stage IV.

Termination. The time comes, of course, in any group's life when the group's work is completed and/or the group needs to terminate. Completion and termination are important ingredients in the life and dynamics of a group. Unfortunately, they are seldom recognized for their importance nor planned for properly. A group needs to have both the capacity and the willingness to finish the task and to move on. Some groups get "stuck" and drag on and on, way beyond their usefulness or effectiveness. Fearful of facing the future without the group, the group members hang on to the past. Also, feeling guilty or unfulfilled in the past, the group may tenaciously hang on to a "hoped-for" future rather than acknowledge the failure and move on. Occasionally, groups get stuck in the now and are so absorbed in the dynamics of each session that they miss any sense of movement toward a goal. On the other hand, there are some groups that terminate prematurely and miss the exciting and important opportunities that could come from continued participation in the group. In any group situation, however, a formal ending is important.

Usually, it is good to give the participants notice of the termination two or three meetings prior to the last session. This gives the participants time to prepare themselves for leaving and eliminates the shock of a sudden announcement of the group's ending (which, incidentally, can often produce feelings of abandonment). There is grief involved in terminating a group. The longer the group has been together, and the greater the value to the participants, the greater the experience of grief will be. This grieving process needs to be identified and openly acknowledged within the group, either person to person or collectively. Group members need to have the opportunity to say their "good-byes." They also need and enjoy having the opportunity to celebrate the group's or their personal completion, its successes, and simply the pleasures of having been together and worked together as a group.

One additional word of caution to the leader. Sometimes the closing celebration is so pleasurable, particularly as the group's successes and accomplishments are reviewed, that the group members ask to continue or to begin again. It is important for the leader not to give in to this very tempting encouragement, but to firmly stay with the decision. Too often, a group that decides at its last meeting to continue on, dies a slow, painful death rather than concluding with a clear, positive ending. Incidentally, because a group terminates does not mean that it can not start again as a new group with a new contract and new goals. However, the leader must allow a group to end when that time is ready.

LEADERSHIP FUNCTIONS AT STAGE IV

Leadership Goal

The final leadership goal is that of effecting a clear and satisfying conclusion and ending of the group.

As we have repeatedly indicated, a developmental framework to an understanding of small groups requires that all of the leadership skills involved in the previous three stages are involved at this final stage. One additional skill is needed as the group ends.

Terminating. It is important, as we have mentioned, to give at least a two-week notice for terminating a group. This gives the members of the group time to think, reflect, and otherwise prepare for the conclusion. There is a grief process that is experienced by people (including the leader) who have been in a group. The recognition of and preparation for (anticipatory grief) the separation, dying, death, and grief process is very helpful for the leader and for the participants as well. Elizabeth Kubler-Ross clearly outlined the emotional process of dying, listing five distinct stages that the dying person goes through: denial, bargaining, anger, depression, and acceptance.[7] Groups will often go through this process as they come to their conclusion. The grief process for the person who has experienced an important loss takes the following steps, according to Richard Obershaw, a grief therapist: protest, despair, detachment, and reorganization.[8] It is, I believe, important for the leader to be aware of this process and to allow it to happen. It is a normal and healthy response to ending something that has been important to a person, and this understanding will lead to a more positive termination of the group.

CONCLUSION

As we finish this manual on the dynamics and leadership of small groups, it is important that the small group leader not be overly self-conscious about these dynamics and skills as they lead or participate in a small group. In the leadership

[7] Elizabeth Kubler-Ross, *On Death and Dying* (New York: Macmillan, 1969).
[8] *Toward Understanding,* a privately published booklet on death, grief, and funerals.

learning process it is useful to have practice experiences. In learning new skills, a leader is often very self-conscious about using those new skills and observing new dynamics. These practice situations often feel rather stilted and awkward (incidentally, it usually seems more awkward to the leader than to those in the group). However, the conscious practice of new skills is helpful in integrating them into one's repertoire of skills. In the ongoing work of small group leadership, it is good for the leader to be natural (genuine) and trust both that leader's intuitive senses and her or his capacity to have spontaneous recall of the dynamics and skills we have discussed. It is good for the leader to be natural, relaxed, and not overly anxious about remembering and doing everything.

Furthermore, it is important to emphasize that the ultimate test of the effectiveness of the strategy, methodology, process, or skills employed is not how well it fits a particular theory or program. Rather, the ultimate test of a leadership style or strategy is whether or not it meets the needs of the group and its individual members. That is to say "Does it work for the participants?" Secondly, "Does it accomplish the purpose(s) for which the group was established?" In the end, while we have listed critical group dynamics and important leadership skills, the important concluding concerns are pragmatic ones—"Has the group accomplished its purpose?" and, "Have the participants benefited from their participation?"

Group dynamics are just that—dynamic—and therefore, hard to pin down or reduce to static statements. Furthermore, group leadership is an art, developed through experience (by trial and error), as well as feedback from group members and other skilled leaders. Also involved is a commitment to being a good artist and an honest, genuine, concerned, and caring person who enjoys his or her work. It is my hope that this book has helped you understand a little more about what happens in groups and how you might become a more skilled artist in leading groups. It is also my hope that you will find your leadership increasingly enjoyable.

(1) As individuals and as a group, is there a task that you need or would like to accept? Is there a risk that would be desirable to take? Set an action goal and develop an action plan, including an evaluation process. In this, and each of the following exercises, the responsibility for leadership should again be rotated.

(2) As a practice group, evaluate the learning experience for each person and for the group as a whole. Discuss the experience each person has had as a result of this course, noting what each person has learned about themselves, their leadership skills, and their awareness of group dynamics. Include in the evaluation an assessment of the specific incidents and behaviors that encouraged a positive learning experience and those that hindered. Include any awareness of subgrouping or interpersonal conflict that emerged.

(3) As an action step and as a formal conclusion, design and execute a concluding celebration to this learning experience with your practice group.

Include in that celebration, specific (concrete!) statements of the new appreciations the participants have for each other as a result of their having shared this experience. Also include a statement from each person about one new or renewed learning or action step they will be taking as a result of this course. Remember, have fun!

Appendix I

I. Adapted from a covenant developed and used by the Action
Training Network, 9606 Euclid Avenue, Cleveland, Ohio,
44106:

I, _____, understand that this group
is a small community of people who meet regularly for a limited
period, to help work on changes in the policies and practices
of an organization.

I can say YES to these interests on my part:

I see my participation as working to change that organization in which I have or could have influence for beneficial
change.

I want the support of others who have a similar view.

I will attend all sessions except in the case of serious emergen-
cies.

I also want to help implement the purpose of my group by:
Accepting responsibility for activities between meetings as re-

lated to my own life style, my support of others in the group,
and my preparation for meetings.
Committing myself to a disciplined group process.

II. We agree with each other to the following:
    1. To attend every session except in case of emergency or illness.
       I consider that time to be the highest priority in my schedule.
    2. Do all reading assignments and answer all questions.
    3. I promise to respect and encourage each of the members
       of the group.
    4. What goes on in this group stays here. I will say nothing
       that can be traced back or that could be injurious or embar-
       rassing to my covenant partners.
    5. You have a right to expect growth from me so that I may
       give you my fullness.

III. Adapted from *Small Group Leaders' Handbook,* prepared by
     Inter-Varsity Christian Fellowship, Madison, Wisconsin: Used
     by permission.

FORMULATING A GROUP COVENANT

A. Definition of a covenant: a formal, solemn, and binding agreement; a written agreement or promise between two or more
   parties for the performance of some action; a pledge or contract.

B. Reasons for having a covenant:
   1. Establishes intentionality
   2. Provides freedom by defining expectations
   3. Provides accountability
   4. Enhances commitment
   5. Serves as a reference for evaluation
   6. Provides a basis for vulnerability

C. When to make a covenant:
   1. Wait until a growing level of trust has been established by
      the group
   2. Caution: too ambitious or exacting a commitment written too
      early in the group's life can be frustrating and produce feelings
      of inadequacy.

D. Types of covenants:
  1. Assumed—each may have an idea, but it is never discussed.
  2. Purchased—details set up by another and someone buys into it (for example, someone joins a group that is already going and accepts the commitments set by those who are already members).
  3. Imposed—directions set by a supervising person or group (the Covenant of Intention you signed before camp is an example of this).
  4. Negotiated—the group agrees together on the ingredients of the covenant (though 1 through 3 are usually in operation when a group begins, 4 is what a group should strive for).

E. Steps of a covenant:
  1. What a covenant is and is not:
     It is not a statement of what an ideal small group is.
     It is the steps this group is willing to take for the growth and edification of the members or for the accomplishment of a mutual task.
  2. Ask the group what their expectations are for the group.
  3. List these so the whole group can see them.
  4. To what are we willing to commit ourselves as a group to meet the expectations?
  5. State the duration and evaluation time for the covenant.
  6. Make sure all agree with each statement and that each part is fully understood by all.
  7. Have the covenant typed up and signed by each member.
  8. Follow through with encouragement, needed training, and evaluation.

F. Ingredients of a group covenant:
  1. Attendance commitment and other ways of being account-able.
  2. Membership—who can join and when.
  3. Duration of commitment—when will we renegotiate?
  4. Length of meetings and content.

Appendix II

This is a sample evaluation sheet for use in a variety of small group meetings. It may be copied or adapted without further permission. Group members should simply be instructed to give their honest and immediate impressions in response to the following questions.

IN THIS MEETING:	(Circle one category for each statement.)			
1. *Leadership was*	Dominated by one person	Dominated by a subgroup	Centered in about half the group	Shared by all members of the group
2. *Communication was*	Badly blocked	Difficult	Fairly open	Very open and free-flowing

[a] from *Groups Alive—Church Alive,* by Clyde Reid, (New York: Harper & Row, 1969), p. 60.

3. *People were* Phony   Hidden   Fairly   Honest and
                                              open   authentic
4. *The group*   Avoiding its   Loafing   Getting   Working
   was   task   some   hard at its
                                              work done   task
5. *I felt*   Misunder-   Somewhat   Somewhat   Completely
                 stood and   misunder-   accepted   accepted
                 rejected   stood   and
                                                            understood
                                                            by the
                                                            group.

6. The one word I would use to describe the climate of this meeting:

_____

7. Suggestions:

_____

_____

_____

ROLE PLAYING SCALE[a]

Date _____ Helper _____ Helpee _____

Watch the helper very carefully and check what you observe. If you see something more than once, check it more than once. The space below is for you to jot down the notes about what you might have seen in the practice session.

Sitting and Movements
____ 1. faces helpee squarely
____ 2. looks at helpee
____ 3. looks away from helpee
____ 4. slouches or sits rigidly erect
____ 5. sits in a relaxed manner
____ 6. nods head
____ 7. shows nervous mannerisms
____ 8. shows distracting gestures
____ 9. show helpful gestures

[a] from *People Helper Growthbook*, by Gary Collins (Santa Ana, California: Vision House, 1976).

____ 10. touches the helpee

____ 11. other _____

Responses

____ 12. asks yes/no questions

____ 13. asks more general questions

____ 14. asks "why?" questions

____ 15. asks a series of questions without pausing for an answer

____ 16. asks probing questions (to get more information)

____ 17. gives reassurance, encourages

____ 18. expresses understanding

____ 19. says "mm-hmmm"

____ 20. gives explanations

____ 21. gives advice

____ 22. gives moral judgments

____ 23. responds to helpee's feelings

____ 24. responds to content statements

____ 25. comments on helpee's behavior

____ 26. is silent

____ 27. confronts

____ 28. other _____

Voice

____ 29. shaky and nervous voice

____ 30. steady and reassuring voice

____ 31. voice too loud

____ 32. voice too soft

____ 33. other _____

Helper Characteristics

____ 34. patient

____ 35. understanding

____ 36. accepting

____ 37. warm and empathetic

____ 38. placable

____ 39. excessively curious

____ 40. other _____

In general, the following are considered to be helpful and desirable responses: 1, 2, 5, 6, 9, 13, 16, 17, 18, 19, 23, 24, 25, 26, 30, 34, 36, and 37.

Notes:

_____

Name of Observer / Evaluator

MEASURING THE CARING ATMOSPHERE
AND HELPFULNESS OF GROUPS

Group Leader's Name _____ Number of Times Attended ____

1. On a scale of 1 to 10, how would you rate the caring atmosphere of the group?

VERY UNCARING			INDIFFERENT				UNUSUALLY HIGH, INTENSIVE CARING		
Cold			*Neutral*				*Warm*		
1	2	3	4	5	6	7	8	9	10

2. On a scale of 1 to 10, how would you rate the helpfulness of the group to you, personally?

UNHELPFUL			NEITHER HELPFUL NOR HARMFUL				VERY HELPFUL		
								Initiated significant personal	
Harmful			*Neutral*				*growth/change*		
1	2	3	4	5	6	7	8	9	10

3. On a scale of 1 to 10, how would you rate the helpfulness of the leaders of your group?

UNHELPFUL			NEITHER HELPFUL NOR HARMFUL				VERY HELPFUL		
								Initiated significant personal	
Harmful			*Neutral*				*growth/change*		
1	2	3	4	5	6	7	8	9	10

4. Rate your group leaders on a scale of 1 to 10 as to the extent to which you sense they accurately understood you

MISUNDER- STOOD ME	AVERAGE UNDERSTANDING	HIGHLY UNDERSTANDING
Didn't *understand* *me at all*	*Same as* *anyone* *else*	*Understood me* *accurately*

1   2   3   4   5   6   7   8   9   10

5. Rate your group leaders as to their authenticity with you as a person.

THEY SEEM LIKE FACES.		THEY ARE HIGHLY AUTHENTIC
Dishonest; *don't know* *themselves*	*Average* *authenticity* *genuineness*	*Unusually* *together,* *genuine & authentic*

1   2   3   4   5   6   7   8   9   10

Appendix III

This is an educational and support group program, seeking to provide a nonthreatening, safe, and accepting atmosphere for sharing and discussion of difficulties in dealing with our emotional lives. We hope to help each other grow in our coping abilities, emotional adjustments, and decision-making processes.

GROUND RULES

1. *Confidentiality*

   We ask only your first name. The problems, successes, and work of each group member are personal and expected to be kept confidential. If you wish to share anything about your group experience outside, we ask that you confine your sharing to what is happening to you.

2. *Freedom of Speech*

   You are free to say or not to say whatever you choose within the bounds of common courtesy. You may request comment or feedback from other group members, but you are not required to accept it unsolicited. We suggest you don't carry unexpressed resentments home, but express uncomfortable feelings that you are aware of.

3. *Mutual Caring*
Mutual caring and concern become an integral part of the group process. When you decide to discontinue participation in the group, for whatever reason, we ask you to let us know, preferably before your last visit, so that we may send you on your way with our good wishes, knowing you will be welcomed back any time you choose.

GUIDELINES FOR BEHAVIOR IN SUPPORT GROUPS

1. *All persons make their own decisions:*
You are not expected to do what someone else wants or thinks should be done.

2. *Everyone is open with the group:*
You are expected to bring concerns, problems, and action possibilities to the group for their conversation.

3. *What is shared within a group is confidential:*
You have a right to expect that what you share will not be retold outside the group.

4. *Members of the group are accountable to and for one another:*
Agreements and commitments are important in groups. You will hold yourselves accountable to follow through and check with one another on agreements made in the group. When you make an action commitment, the group helps you check on progress along the way.

5. *Members of the group are encouraged to express themselves out of their diversity:*
Every member of a group is unique and different. Each has a different way of thinking, expressing feelings, acting for change, and so on. You will come to value these different perspectives. The richness of difference in a group is stimulating and brings more possibilities to the solving of problems.

6. *Members of the group work together in the development of shared values:*

   In a group, we are continually examining and sharing with each other the values that we feel are important. Over time, we will begin to discover common values to which we are committed. This takes time to develop, however, and is not assumed. It can grow only out of an active sharing and exploration of differences.

7. *Members of the group have fun together:*

   Having fun and relaxing together is one way of building a sense of community and support. A support group finds occasions to celebrate events in members' lives and sharing in their success and failures.

8. *Membership in the group changes over time:*

   As we grow, or as our situations change, some of us may come to feel that the group is no longer a source of support. If the commitment is to helping each member grow, these feelings will be thoroughly expressed and explored within the group, so that we are supported even in a decision to move out of the group. At some point, the group may decide to disband. If feelings are shared and explored, this also can be done in a spirit of goodwill.

Bibliography

Group Counseling, Psychotherapy, and Dynamics

BERNE, ERIC, *Principles of Group Treatment*, New York: Grove Press, 1966.

DIEDRICH, RICHARD C., *Group Procedures: Purposes, Processes and Outcomes;* selected readings for the counselor, Boston: Houghton-Mifflin, 1972.

EGAN, GERARD, *Encounter Groups: Group Processes for Interpersonal Growth*, Belmont, California: Brooks/Cole, 1970.

_____, *Interpersonal Living;* A skills-contact approach to human relations training in groups, Monterey, California: Brooks/Cole, 1976.

GAZDA, George M., *Group Counseling: A Developmental Approach* (2nd ed.), Boston: Allyn and Bacon, 1978.

HILL, WILLIAM FAWCETT, *Hill Interaction Matrix*, Los Angeles: Youth Study Center, University of Southern California, 1965.

JACOBS, ALFRED and WILFORD SPRADLIN, *The Group As Agent of Change*, New York: Behavioral Publications, 1974. Theories and applications of group intervention methods to effect change.

JOHNSON, DAVID W. and FRAND P. JOHNSON, *Joining Together: Group Therapy and Group Skills*, Englewood Cliffs, N.J.: Prentice-Hall, 1975.

LUFT, JOSEPH, *Group Process*, Palo Alto: Mayfield Publications, 1970.

ROGERS, CAROL, *Carl Rogers on Encounter Groups*, New York: Harper & Row, 1970.

THOMSON, SHEILA, *The Group Process As a Helping Technique*, Oxford, New York: Pergamon Press, 1970.

YALOM, IRVIN D., *The Theory and Practice of Group Psychotherapy* (2nd ed.), New York: Basic Books, 1975.

Groups in Church Settings

CASTEEL, JOHN, *Spiritual Renewal Through Personal Groups*, New York: Association Press, 1957.

CLINEBELL, HOWARD, *Growth Groups*, Nashville: Abingdon, 1975. First published as *The People Dynamic*, New York: Harper & Row, 1972.

EVANS, LOUIS H., JR., *Creative Love*, Old Tappan, N.J.: Revell, 1977.

KNOWLES, JOSEPH W., *Group Counseling*, Englewood Cliffs, N.J.: Prentice-Hall, 1964.

OMAN, JOHN B., *Group Counseling in the Church: A Practical Guide for Lay Counselors*, Minneapolis: Augsburg, 1972.

REID, CLYDE, *Groups Alive—Church Alive*, New York: Harper & Row, 1969.

WIEBE, MICHAEL, *Small Groups: Getting Them Started, Keeping Them Going*, Madison, Wisconsin: Inter-Varsity Christian Fellowship, 1976.

Task-Oriented Groups

BORMANN, ERNEST G. and NANCY G. BORMANN, *Effective Small Group Communication*, Minneapolis: Burgess Publishing, 1972.

GUTHRIE, EILEEN and WARREN SAM MILLER, *Making Change: A Guide to Effectiveness in Groups*, Minneapolis: Interpersonal Communication Programs, Inc., 1978.

Business and Organizational Management

BUCKLEY, W., *Sociology and Modern Systems Theory*, Englewood Cliffs, N.J.: Prentice-Hall, 1967.

BUSKIRK, RICHARD H., *Modern Management and Machiavelli*, New York: Mentor Executive Library, 1974.

LEAVITT, HAROLD J., *Managerial Psychology: An Introduction to Individuals, Pairs, and Groups in Organizations* (3rd ed.), Chicago: University of Chicago Press, 1972.

SCHEIN, EDGAR and WARREN G. BENNIS, *Personal and Organizational Change Through Group Methods: The Laboratory Approach*, New York: Wiley, 1967.

SCOTT, WILLIAM G. and TERRANCE R. MITCHELL, *Organizational Theory: A Structural and Behavioral Analysis* (3rd ed.), Homewood, Illinois: Richard D. Irwin, 1976.

Sisk, Henry L., *Principles of Management: A Systems Approach to the Management Process,* n.p.: Southern-Western Publications, 1969.

Townsend, Robert, *Up the Organization,* New York: Alfred A. Knopf, 1970.

Groups in Education

Bennett, Margaret E., *Guidance and Counseling in Groups* (2nd ed.), New York: McGraw-Hill, 1963.

Flynn, Elizabeth W. and John F. Lafaso, *Group Discussion as Learning Process: A Sourcebook,* New York: Paulist Press, 1972.

Martin, Robert J., "Encouraging a Sense of Group Through Group Discussion," Chapter 10, *Teaching Through Encouragement,* Englewood Cliffs, N.J.: Prentice-Hall, 1980.

Sharan, Shlomo and Yael Sharan, *Small Group Teaching,* Englewood Cliffs, N.J.: Educational Technology Publications, 1976.

Counseling Skills

Benjamin, Alfred. *The Helping Interview* (2nd ed.), Boston: Houghton-Mifflin, 1974.

Brammer, L.M., *The Helping Relationship: Process and Skills,* Englewood Cliffs, N.J.: Prentice-Hall, 1973.

Bullmer, Kenneth, *The Art of Empathy:* A manual for improving accuracy interpersonal perception, New York: Human Sciences Press, 1975.

Carkhuff, Robert R., *Helping and Human Relations,* Vol. I & II, New York: Holt, Rinehart and Winston, 1969.

  The Art of Helping III, Amherst, Massachusetts: Human Resource Development Press, 1977.

  The Art of Helping IV, Amherst, Massachusetts: Human Resource Development Press, 1980.

Collins, Gary, *How to Be a People Helper,* Santa Ana, California: Vision House, 1976.

Egan, Gerard, *The Skilled Helper,* Monterey, California: Brooks/Cole, 1975.

_____, *Exercises in the Skilled Helper,* Monterey, California: Brooks/Cole, 1975.

Communication Skills

Gordon, Thomas, *Parent Effectiveness Training,* Chapters 3 through 7, New York: Wyden, 1970.

Johnson, David W., *Reaching Out: Interpersonal effectiveness and self-actualization,* Englewood Cliffs, N.J.: Prentice-Hall, 1972.

MILLER, SHERROD and ELAM NUNNALLY, DANIEL WACKMAN, *Alive and Aware: Improving Communication in Relationships,* Minneapolis: Interpersonal Communication Programs, Inc., 1975.

————, *Talking Together,* Minneapolis: Interpersonal Communication Programs, Inc., 1979.

————, *Working Together,* Minneapolis: Interpersonal Communication Programs, Inc., 1980.

————, and CAROL SALINE, *Straight Talk,* New York: Rawson-Wade Publishers, Inc., 1981.

STEVENS, JOHN O., *Awareness: Exploring, Experimenting, Experiencing,* Moab, Utah: Real People Press, 1971.

Family Systems

ALDOUS, JOAN, *Family Careers,* New York: Wiley and Sons, 1978.

BARNARD, CHARLES P. and RAMON CORRALES, *The Theory and Technique of Family Therapy,* Springfield, Illinois: Charles C Thomas, 1979.

CARNES, PATRICK J., *Understanding Us,* Minneapolis: Interpersonal Communication Programs, Inc., 1981.

HALEY, JAY, *Problem-Solving Therapy,* New York: Harper & Row, 1976.

MINUCHEN, SALVADOR, *Families and Family Therapy,* Cambridge, Massachusetts: Harvard University Press, 1974.

SATIR, VIRGINIA, *Peoplemaking,* Palo Alto, California: Science and Behavior Books, 1972.

INDEX